Jesus, Unleashed

Joel M. Killion

inner life
MEDIA
Wilson, North Carolina

Jesus, Unleashed

By Joel M. Killion

Published by:
Inner Life Media
www.InnerLifeMinistries.com
Wilson, North Carolina

All Scripture quotations include a description of the translation or paraphrase used.

ISBN: 978-0-578-06268-6

Printed in the United States of America
First Printing

Contents

Acknowledgements

I want to thank my Mom who sacrificed far more than can be expressed to raise me and my brother as she was directed by the Lord. Thank you. I love you mom.

Finally, I want to thank my wife for being the best part of my life. She has shared me with the Lord since the day we met and has been gracious to me at all times. She is my friend and I want to dedicate this work to her. She is my sister and my spouse, my lover and my companion. There is no one like her. I love you babe.

Dedication

To "the Voice of One" who spoke Life into my life from day one through many oracles in the presence of many witnesses. You're my best friend.

Introduction

When a veil is removed, it doesn't create something that has never existed before; it simply reveals what was always there. To see Jesus more and more clearly requires the removal of all the veils that stand between us and him. Yet, when they are withdrawn, they don't create a new Jesus but simply reveal the one who was always there. What you are about to read will seem, at times, new, but remember it's only new to you.

As you progressively move closer and closer to knowing him as he knows you, you will mature beyond the elementary principles of Christ to the more advanced, which will change you from the inside out into who you really are and have actually always been in him (Hebrews 5:12-6:1).

Whatever questions you have about who you are or why you're alive can be answered in one way and one way only: by seeing Jesus. To the degree that we see him, we are like him. To the degree that we are like him, we re-present him. Therefore, our greatest need is to have a fuller, more accurate, more intimate knowledge of who Jesus really is, deep inside, without all the mess we've accumulated from being exposed to and scripted by religious systems and man-made traditions. But, if our revelation of Jesus doesn't make us more like him, it's all for nothing, leaving us with external standards without internal transformation.

Our lack of revelation regarding who Jesus really was (and still is) has enabled us to make him whatever we want (Proverbs 29:18). And who he is to us means everything.

Who Are We Following?

I've often wondered if Paul the apostle would be happy to know that the 21st century church has patterned itself more after him than Jesus. And what about Peter, James, John, and Jude? What about every Christian leader in church history? What would they think? Of course, it's noble to imitate those who have followed Jesus but wouldn't it be better to imitate Jesus himself? Do we want to follow followers of Jesus, or do we want to follow Jesus?

> Do we want to follow followers of Jesus, or do we want to follow Jesus?

When we say we're a Christian, what are we saying? How do we define what it means? When we think of Christianity, most think of church, doctrines, religion, the Bible, Christian television, door-to-door evangelism, etc. But Jesus was so much more than these things. And yet after he ascended, well-meaning human hearts motivated by religious zeal and "good ideas," started changing his legacy, stretching, bending and deflating his life, throughout the next 2000 years, leaving us with a brand of Christianity that is Christless at best and doesn't resemble him at all. I call this dead religion: a form of piety that denies the power of Jesus' real life. Of course, we've all been bitten and poisoned by this slippery snake; we've all believed the lies and perhaps still do. And now, by today's standards, we're all "good Christians" living the "good Christian life." But this is changing as more and more people are giving up their good Christian lives and following Christ who alone defines true Christianity.

There is a massive difference between Christianity as Jesus lived it and Christianity as it is today. No longer should we allow anyone or anything to define his life for us. No longer should we allow other so-called Christians to define the reality and beauty of what it means to be a true friend and follower of Jesus. No longer should we allow mainstream Christianity, Christian television, Vacation Bible School, Christian literature, or professional ministers, as good as they may be, to explain or interpret the kind of life he meant for us.

Jesus is the only foundation worth building upon. The Book of Acts and the epistles are not the foundation of the true Christian life and cannot withstand the glory of that which needs to be built upon it. The apostolic writings of the New Testament must be measured by and built on the life of Jesus as seen in the Gospels; we must see their letters and revelations through Jesus' teachings and not the other way around. His words and deeds communicate the greatest wisdom and the most powerful truths of all time. He is the mark for the prize of the High Calling (Philippians 3:14). And anything we see, hear, or believe that does not agree with the essence of Jesus' life and ministry should be re-examined.

> Jesus is the only foundation worth building upon.

Of course, there are many things about the Lord that we do not understand, and that is okay. What's important is that we see Jesus who is the image of God and who alone will show us the Father. So, let us follow the advice that Martin Luther gave his students: "let us flee the hidden God and run to Jesus Christ."

As Fyodor Dostoevsky once said, "If anyone proved to me that Christ was outside the truth...then I would prefer to remain with Christ than with the truth." Jesus is the only divine pattern by which every doctrine, belief, or revelation should be measured and tested as we mature into his exact likeness and image; there is simply no other justifiable model for the true Christian life.

Re-thinking Jesus

How is it that the church has, in Dorothy Sayers' words, "very efficiently pared the claws of the Lion of Judah" and "certified

Him as a fitting household pet for pale curates and pious old ladies"?

We've all, in one way or another, brought the Word of God down to our level of experience, rather than raised our expectations to the level of his Word. In other words, we've lowered Jesus' idea of "normal" down to our own and been left with a brand of Christianity that is in our own image, that has been restricted by our own affections.

We've settled for another Jesus and another Gospel (2 Corinthians 11:2-4; Galatians 1:6-9). We've mixed and matched our personal religious beliefs, ideals, and preferences, which vary like the stars, and sewed them together to produce a patchwork, "Designer Jesus." And now, you can have your Jesus, and I can have mine, and it doesn't matter if our versions of him contradict each other; it's all relative, right?

But what would Jesus think if he appeared on this planet today in human form and saw what we've turned him into? If he came face to face with our version of him, would he approve? And, in the end, would our "new and improved" Jesus not say more about us than about him?

When we read the Gospels, we don't read them as they actually are but as we are, interpreting things through our own culture and experiences. We have our own maps, models, rulers, and scales, and he doesn't fit any of them. And so often, because we dislike (fear) anything different, we unwittingly abandon or dilute him to feel better about what we don't know or can't explain. Then we follow him as far as we understand, subjecting him to our mainstream wisdom which often masquerades as "Gospel Truth." But who are we to restrict him to what we think or understand?

When the enemy comes in, the Lord always raises up a standard, like a flood, against him. But unfortunately, the Lord often does so alone because very few "believers" are willing to truly let him live through them, as he really is, despite their beliefs about him. If your faith is in him but your view of him is limited, your faith will be limited as well. If you want to work the works of God, to do his will, you must believe in the one he sent, not the one you think you know (John 6:28-29). Only then will his standard be raised again the enemy.

It's time to start from scratch, from the ground up. It's time to renew our minds on the cellular level. Many of our traditional views of Jesus make us old wineskins that cannot be used by him until our minds are transformed.

> Many of our traditional views of Jesus make us old wineskins that cannot be used by him until our minds are transformed.

So, as you read this book, keep the following points in mind:

- True Christians resemble Jesus, not other Christians or a pastor or a church or a ministry or anything else. He alone is to be our "magnificent obsession."
- What we believe about Jesus will influence the way we live in every way, depending on how we see him and what we think about him. Our paradigms about him will also affect how we relate to him and the Godhead, how we worship, how we interact with one another and the Kingdom, how we see ourselves, how we believe, what we believe, and will ultimately determine our potential in life, both in this world and the world to come.
- Jesus is not some distant, historical, glow-in-the-dark bronze figure that we cannot relate to. If you have given your life entirely to him, then you are one with him (1 Corinthians 6:17; Hebrews 2:11-13). If you are reborn in Christ then you are a child of the Father and Jesus is your

eldest brother (John 1:12-13; Acts 17:28-29; Hebrews 2:10). If your life is his, then this is who you are. You are a new creation (2 Corinthians 5:17). As the offspring of God, your spiritual identity is more real than who you are naturally. Jesus is your brother more than any natural sibling you may have. And God is more your father and mother than your natural parents or any parental figure you've ever had. This is your heritage, your birthright, despite what you think or feel. And only those who believe, will follow his example and succeed him by doing what he did and more (John 14:12).

- Jesus' life must be the watermark by which we define love, faith, humility, kindness, devotion, and every other virtue. Otherwise, we will find ourselves becoming anything but a true Christian.

Each chapter in this book focuses on some of the many parts of Jesus' life that have caught my attention over the last few years. Needless to say, no other study has so transformed my thinking and my life like this one. Every time I see him, I somehow know and see my true self – who I really am – more and more clearly. Why? Because we came from our Father, which, as a revelation by itself, blows me away every time I think about it. And everything I see and hear is filtered through this ever-expanding awareness of who he is and who I am because of him and drives me beyond the limitations of my predecessors to experience what has been considered impossible by my contemporaries. Something about Jesus brings out the pioneer in me and everyone who has the courage to give him their full, undivided attention. Of course, this is all a process, but now more than ever before, I feel safe and secure in the simplicity of devotion to him and him alone. All the bunny-trails, party-lines and doctrinal fads no longer appeal to me; somehow, they all seem so silly and trite compared to him.

What you are about to read will rock you and may offend you. But, please, before you pass judgment, before you put it down, press through your negative reactions and keep reading. If you give it a full and open-minded hearing, it may surprise you. The choice is yours.

As you read on, be prayerful. Ask Jesus to show you who he is, through his eyes, not yours. Ask him to reduce you to pure and simple devotion to him. As you return to the Gospels – studying them for your own sake – with a passion to know him better, the fog will lift and the sunshine will break through. And as you press on, remember, a search for Jesus is invariably one's own search.

- 1 -

Beneath the Flesh

I told my mom that I wanted to blow my brains out. I thought I was stupid. At least that's what my teachers, class-mates, and so-called friends thought, and somehow what they thought of me seemed to matter more than it ever should have. But I didn't know any better. I was seven years old and very impressionable. I didn't meet the standards of the traditional educational system. I didn't read or count or rhyme like my peers. I didn't socialize, dress and carry myself like everyone else. So, to them, I was missing the mark. In their eyes, I was failing. And I didn't know who I was enough to know that I could ignore their opinions. I guess I thought their positions of power and influence or their roles as "my friends," made them more qualified than anyone, including me, to measure me; and I certainly didn't think to consider Jesus' take on me, even though he was the only one who was ever truly qualified to appraise me.

It seems I didn't meet the standards of anyone who expected me to be someone I wasn't, to be like all my peers. And if it hadn't been for the Lord who led my parents to take me and my brother out of public school to homeschool us, I may have become exactly what everyone "out there" wanted me to be. Who knows? But Jesus knew what he was doing. He put me and my brother in a place where we would be conditioned by Him to live completely unafraid of being who he made us to be – nothing more, nothing less. For the next eleven years, we were encouraged to follow our passions and dreams; we were allowed to think outside every box that everyone "out there" believed in. We were taught to ignore the pull of the world that always seeks to pressure us to conform and comply or else.

And believe it or not, we experienced this worldly pressure in the church more than anywhere else. It was like another world that made the rest of the world look good. And it didn't matter what church we went to; they were all the same even though they said they weren't. They all expected what we couldn't deliver as long as we were ourselves. And it wasn't hard to disappoint them because they were always weighing us in their souls, waiting for us to say something or do something that didn't fit their mold just right. I remember feeling like there was always an elephant in the room hounding me simply because I was different. They seemed to pity me because I didn't have what they had or didn't believe like they believed. I never had all the nice clothes, and when I turned sixteen I didn't have the best car, which only confirmed, in their eyes, how deprived and sheltered I really was. Of course, I never bought into their way of thinking because I could see right through it all, so I just kept being me. When we had Bible study, I asked questions that made the leaders cringe inside – they never could answer my questions – and I made comments that crossed their favorite doctrines; to many of them, I was deceived. When the unpopular were being ridiculed, I defended them, which always made me the new target. When I could muster the courage, I prayed for the sick and hurting, knowing they didn't believe in divine healing or miracles. And as I grew in the Lord and in life, I became more and more free. Of course, I had times when I thought it would be easier to give up and give in and there were times when I did. And, for a time, it was easier, but it never lasted because something in me, like an eagle in a cage, wanted to break out and fly. I had a fire in my bones, and the longer I held it inside, the more it hurt – it even sometimes hurt my physical body. So I bailed, until eventually I became so free that I just let go. I stopped apologizing for being me. I stopped letting what other people think about me be more important than what my Best Friend thinks of me. I quit caring about the status quo and

> "He who joyfully marches to music in rank and file has already earned my contempt. He has been given a large brain by mistake, since for him the spinal cord would fully suffice."
> (Einstein)

10

political correctness. The steely gazes and cold shoulders became more and more irrelevant to me.

I've often loved the quote from Albert Einstein which says, "He who joyfully marches to music in rank and file has already earned my contempt. He has been given a large brain by mistake, since for him the spinal cord would fully suffice." And I like this one too: "Great spirits have always found violent opposition from mediocre minds. The latter cannot understand it when a man does not thoughtlessly submit...but honestly and courageously uses his intelligence."

From the beginning, I've always been fascinated with the people in history, like Einstein, who were radical non-conformists, who swam upstream and defied every limitation that everyone tried to bind them to. People like William Wallace, Abraham Lincoln, Evan Roberts, John G. Lake, Dietrich Bonhoeffer, Winston Churchill, J.R.R. Tolkien, Ronald Reagan, Rush Limbaugh, and others like them have always inspired me to be me. Something inside me loved their stories, their sufferings, and their successes, and I still do. I love their journeys. To me, their lives seem more valuable than all the cookie-cutter masses since the beginning of time.

And yet there has always been one person who has been my primary "role model," my "idol," the one I knew was greater than everyone I'd ever heard of or read about. I knew this man knew everything I had ever felt – good, bad, and ugly – and knew how to overcome all the odds to be who he was born to be. So I studied his life and found my own, and the clearer he became, the more I knew myself. Now, I no longer have to question who I am. All my masks are in the trash. I don't have to waver between being me and being what everyone else wants me to be. I have been given permission to be like him.

He was bold, confident, strong, and true, and no one could shake him. There was nothing in him that anyone could exploit, not even Satan (Luke 4:1-12; John 14:30). He was grounded, not wishy-washy, double-minded, and confused, and he made distinctions like no one else. But it was who he was on the inside, at his core, that made him like this.

What you are about to read is a portion of what I have found about Jesus that has made me new in so many ways and is still being worked into my life. I say a portion because I can't possibly explain the depths to which his identity has affected my own. He has influenced me and is still influencing me in many ways that are far beyond my understanding.

I haven't been able to find anyone like him. At times, I've thought that he is too high, too great, too wonderful to emulate, but, then again, why would I want to lower the bar to what I think is doable? Why settle for second or third best when his life is the best there is and ever will be?

What if we knew who we are just as he knew who he was? Would we not live very different lives? Would we continue to let even one percent of our lives be moved by anyone else? What was Jesus' secret to such an amazing life? Do you really want to know?

The Word Made Flesh

When Jesus came out of the water at his baptism, the heavens opened, and a voice said, *"This is my son, my beloved, in whom I delight!"*

Jesus' spent his first 30 years *"doing"* nothing, as the world understands it, but the first thing we hear about him, out of his daddy's mouth, is how proud he is of his boy. Before he ever preached one *"sermon"* or worked one miracle, he had our papa's approval. His significance never came from his behavior, performance, or achievements. He didn't have to *"earn"* his father's praise or affection. He didn't need the next three years to become significant. He already was.

Then, after hearing his father's words of love for him, Jesus was led into the desert by the Holy Spirit where his metal – his identity and nature - was tested by fire, by Satan himself; when Satan tried to get him to question who he was, Jesus didn't say, *"I know who I am."* Rather, he said, *"It is written... "* or, as he would say today, *"My daddy said..."* Thus, Jesus never relied on his own self-knowledge, on what he thought about himself.

After passing the test, he returned to his hometown and went to church on "Sunday morning"; he approached the *"pulpit,"* was given the scroll of the book of Isaiah, opened it, and read the following:

"The Spirit of the Lord [is] upon Me, because he has anointed Me [the Anointed one, the Messiah] to preach the good news (the Gospel) to the poor; he has sent Me to announce release to the captives and recovery of sight to the blind, to send forth as delivered those who are oppressed [who are downtrodden, bruised, crushed, and broken down by calamity], to proclaim the accepted and acceptable year of the Lord [the day when salvation and the free favors of God profusely abound.]." (Isaiah 61:1-2, Amp)

When he finished reading, he gave the scroll back to the attendant and sat down. Then, with all eyes on him, he said, *"Today this Scripture is fulfilled..."* In other words, he said, *"Today, this Scripture has come to pass, and here I am, the Anointed one, the Messiah, 'the Word made flesh,' before your very eyes."*

Naturally, this confused everyone who heard him because they thought, *"Hold on! This doesn't make any sense! Isn't this guy Joseph and Mary's boy from down the road? How can he be the Messiah?"* He then assured them that they wouldn't receive him for who he really was because no prophet is accepted in his own hometown ("Familiarity breeds contempt"). Then, to make matters worse, he mentioned the ministries of two incredible prophets who were highly respected in Israel's history – Elijah and Elisha – putting himself on their level. This immediately filled everyone with so much anger that they threw him out of the *"church,"* kicked him out of town, and dragged him to a high cliff where they tried, without success, to throw him to his doom (Luke 4:1-30).

These two events – at Jordan and the *"church"* - sparked the beginning of Jesus' public life and ministry. He was openly affirmed by his father and believed it so much that he made his identity the subject of his first *"sermon"* which almost got him killed by his first *"congregation."* His audacious claims about himself posed the dividing point between reality and everything everyone had ever held dear.

In his famous book, <u>Mere Christianity</u>, C. S. Lewis makes this statement: *"Christ says that He is 'humble and meek' and we believe Him; not noticing that, if He were merely a man, humility and meekness are the very last characteristics we could attribute to some of His sayings. I am trying here to prevent anyone saying the really foolish thing that people often say about Him: 'I'm ready to accept Jesus as a great moral teacher, but I don't accept His claim to be God.' That is the one thing we must not say. A man who was merely a man and said the sort of things Jesus said would not be a great moral teacher. He would either be a lunatic--on a level with the man who says he is a poached egg--or else he would be the Devil of Hell. You must make your choice. Either this man was, and is, the Son of God: or else a madman or something worse. You can shut Him up for a fool, you can spit at Him and kill Him as a demon; or you can fall at His feet and call*

Him Lord and God. But let us not come with any patronizing nonsense about His being a great human teacher. He has not left that open to us. He did not intend to."

Jesus didn't have an identity crisis like so many of us, even though he was a human being, made a little lower than the angels, just like us (Hebrews 2:9, 17-18; 4:14-5:2, 7-9; Psalm 8:4-5; Philippians 2:5-8). He never temporized or waffled about himself. He knew who he was, where he came from, why he was here, and where he was going, and most didn't like it (John 4:10, 25-26; 8:14, 23; 18:36-37). His perception of reality determined his identity. His life was established on the Word of God; that is, he was the byproduct of His daddy's affirming words. He didn't entangle himself with the affairs of this life (2 Timothy 2:4-5). He lived before the bar of God (Galatians 1:20) as the Word made flesh, the epistle of God, written on a tablet of flesh for all to read (2 Corinthians 3:1-3).

He also knew who he wasn't – he knew his limits - because you cannot know who you are without also knowing who you aren't. He knew he was not of this world even though he lived in it with everyone else (John 17:14). He knew he was not an earthly king and that his Kingdom was not of this world (John 18:36-37). And when you're that liberated, that self-aware, that settled, only then can you truly live.

Public Persona

Jesus' fame grew with every miracle, sign, and wonder he performed, but his personal value wasn't moved, good or bad, by the approval or disapproval of others (Matthew 4:23-25; John 5:41-44). Some loved him, but most did not. Nevertheless, he wasn't encouraged by praise or discouraged by rejection (Luke 18:18-19; John 5:44; 12:43). He wasn't happy when the crowds were big and sad when they were small, as if numbers had anything to do with his success or failure; in fact, there were times when the crowds grew so large that he would purposefully thin them out by either saying offensive things, climbing mountains, or crossing lakes (Matthew 8:18-22, John 6). When people approached him, wanting to follow him, he would shock them with impossible conditions and many times, let them walk away discouraged (Matthew 19:16-30; Mark 10:17-31; Luke 9:57-62; 18:18-30). His idea of discipleship was nothing like ours (Matthew 7:13-14; 10:25-33; Luke 13:22-30; 14:25-35).

His disciples were never bored because they never knew, moment to moment, what he was going to say or do. He was a mystery-man, an enigma, a walking riddle. He was neither boring nor predictable. He never said or did anything the same way all the time. He was spontaneous and quick to change whatever preconceived ideas everyone had.

For instance, in Mark 3, Jesus and his disciples went to a house (probably Peter's), where they were immediately overwhelmed by a crowd that was pressing upon them with such force that they could not even eat their meal (v. 20). Now, it isn't clear what happened in that house. All we know for sure is that Jesus suddenly began displaying bizarre behavior while he was *"driving out demons"* (verse 22). Then when his family and the disciples heard what he was doing, they went to take him *"by force"* to get him under control (v.21, Amp). According to different translations of the Bible, those who were present thought Jesus had *"lost his senses"* (New American Standard Bible), was *"beside Himself"* (King James Version), *"out of his mind"* (New International Version), went *"crazy"* (Worldwide English New Testament) and got *"carried away with himself"* (The Message Bible). The Wycliffe New Testament says he *"turned into madness."* The original Greek says he was *"out of His wits, insane or bewitched"* (Strong's #1839). Moreover, the scribes and teachers of the law, after observing his behavior, accused him of being possessed by Satan and said that he was casting out demons because he was himself possessed by the prince of demons (verse 22-23). Evidently, Jesus was not *"himself,"* at least from everyone's point of view; in fact, from the religious crowd's view, he was acting more like someone who was demon-possessed than someone who was merely crazy. Of course, we know that Jesus wasn't really possessed by Satan but we can see from this that he did at times do crazy things that didn't look right, that disturbed everyone's religious apple-cart.

This reminds me of the 120 believers in Acts 2 who were accused by onlookers of being drunk, when in fact they were simply responding to the activity of the Holy Spirit. Clearly, Jesus and his followers didn't value respectability over the operations of the Kingdom. Those who only observed things on the surface never saw the true value of what was really happening; they were merely offended by methods and appearances from their limited points of reference. Only those who had the humility to see the heart of the matter were able to see what God was really doing beyond what they experienced with their five natural senses.

> His pattern of behavior disappointed all who sought a *"conventional"* leader.

As Philip Yancey stated in <u>The Jesus I Never Knew</u>, Jesus' *"...Searing honesty made him seem downright tactless in some settings. Few people felt comfortable around him; those who did were the type no one else felt comfortable around. He was notoriously difficult to predict, pin down, or even understand."*

There were many times when he insulted, tested, or refused those who were desperate for help or advice (Matthew 15:22-26; 17:17; John 4:46-48). At other times he only healed one person in a great multitude, leaving the rest uncured (John 5:1-9; Luke 4:25-27). When his good friend Lazarus was sick, he didn't heal him but let him die and didn't raise him from the dead until four days later (John 11:1-44). Needless to say, His pattern of behavior disappointed all who sought a *"conventional"* leader.

Jesus didn't play to people and had no desire to make a name for himself (Philippians 2:7). He was so secure in himself that he actually discouraged those he had healed from telling anyone about what he had done for them (Matthew 8:1-4; 9:30; 12:16; Mark 1:44; 8:22-30). And again, when he was transfigured before Peter, James and John, he told them not to tell what they had seen to anyone, until his resurrection (Matthew 17:9).

On another occasion, when the annual Feast of Tabernacles – one of the greatest events of the year – was near in Jerusalem, Jesus stayed in Galilee. But his brothers protested, "...*You ought to leave here and go to Judea, so that your disciples may see the miracles you do. No one who wants to become a public figure acts in secret. Since you are doing these things, show yourself to the world.*" But the reason his brothers said this was because they didn't really believe in him; if they had, they would have known that he had no desire to "*show*" himself to the world as a well-known "*public figure*" – he didn't have to (John 7:1-6, NIV). There was no supernatural glow about him, no halo. There was nothing in his appearance that attracted anyone (Isaiah 53:2-3). He spurned the spotlight, distrusted crowds and public opinion, and spent most of his time in towns of small size and little importance.

At times it seemed as if the whole world was going after him (Matthew 21:1-11; Mark 11:1-11; Luke 19:28-40; John 12:1-19); then it would turn on him, hating him and seeking his death (Matthew 10:22; John 7:7; 15:18, 24-25). In many ways it seems the masses were bipolar and schizophrenic, shouting "*Hosanna*" one week and yelling "*crucify him*" the next. But this never took Jesus by surprise because he knew who they really were. When his disciples, his own home-town and even his own family members including his cousin John the Baptist, doubted or were offended at him, he wasn't bothered as if their opinions mattered (Matthew 11:2-6; 13:10, 53-58; 15:12; Mark 6:1-6; Luke 7:18-23). He knew the futility of their thoughts, and he knew their true nature, which is why he never allowed himself to be moved by them; he never committed or entrusted himself to anyone (John 2:23-25; 1 Corinthians 3:20). If he had, he would never have been truly free.

Jesus' focus was so entirely upon the Kingdom and the things of the Kingdom that those who were of a different mind were constantly bothered by him. He offended and insulted the masses (Luke 11:29; 12:54-59; John 6), terrified and confused his disciples (Matthew 14:26; 15:15-20; 16:5-11, 24), and upset religious leaders, scribes, and lawyers (Matthew 15:1-14; 16:1-4; 19:1-12; 21:33-46; 22:15-32; 23; Luke 11:37-54). At one time or another, he managed to mystify and alienate every major group in Palestine. And to make matters worse, he was known by many, including his family, as an insane, blaspheming, demon-possessed, troublemaking, wine-bibbing, non-conforming disturber of the peace who wrote in the dirt with his finger and hung-out with the riff-raff of society (Matthew 3:20-22; 9:3, 34; 11:18-19; Luke 7:33-35; John 7:20; 8:48-49, 52; 10:20-21).

On one occasion when Jesus entered into Jerusalem, the entire city became agitated and began *"trembling with excitement,"* asking, *"Who is this?"* (Matthew 21:10-11, Amp). This was a common occurrence with him, and yet he wasn't moved. His confidence wasn't shaken when he was banished from villages, towns, cities, or regions (Mark 5:13-20). He knew who he was, despite others, and no one could take that from him. He wasn't troubled when people interrupted his messages, questioned his authority, tested his wisdom, ridiculed his good name, or rejected him altogether (Matthew 9:18, 24; 21:23-27; 11:27-33; Luke 20). It didn't matter that most overlooked or stiff-armed him before they ever really knew him. He was the sweet fragrance of life to the needy but an aroma of death to those who were dead in self-satisfaction.

He failed every known classification and did not fit anyone's expectations of *"the coming Messiah."* As C. S. Lewis put it, *"He was not at all like the psychologist's picture of the integrated, balanced, adjusted, happily married, employed, popular citizen. You can't really be very well 'adjusted' to your world if it says you 'have a devil' and ends by nailing you up naked to a stake of wood."* All too often we tend to believe that Jesus was normal, but what is normal? What if normal in his world is abnormal or even crazy in ours? How could anyone easily accept him when he made himself far too easy to reject?

> He was the first to experience what has always been available for every child of God.

What's funny to me is that no one knew who he was except the demons who always recognized him as the "Holy one of God" or "Son of the Most High." They clearly had more discernment than those who heard his words and saw his works everyday, and they recognized him better than all the religious leaders combined; this is why they knew his presence and obeyed his every word without question (Matthew 8:28-34; Mark 1:21-26, 34; 5:1-13).

Relationship

Who we are, on the inside, is often shaped by the influences of our world around us (family, friends, books, mentors, media, etc.) and determines our level of faith, confidence and leadership which guides our whole life for good or evil. But there's a higher way!

A wise man once said, *"Tell me whom you love, and I will tell you who you are."* Jesus *was* who he loved. His whole being was wrapped up in his father, the love of his life, who influenced him and made him who he was. In other words, he wasn't shaped from without, but from within, where his father lived.

No one had ever known God like Jesus did which explains why he was the first to live the kind of life he lived. Nowhere in human history had anyone ever called God *"father,"* let alone "*my father*," but Jesus did (Matthew 7:21; Luke 10:22; John 8:19; 20:17). In a time when God was known as being distant and ineffable, when Jews never dared to pronounce his Name, Jesus called him "*Abba*" (A familiar Aramaic term of family affection, likened to "*daddy*," the first word many children spoke). Jesus was the first to apply such a word to Yahweh. This, of course, set a new precedent for relationship with the God of Abraham, Isaac, and Jacob. Unlike so many of us, he didn't identify himself with his blood-kin or natural heritage; his papa was his heritage, his real blood-kin, his only source of security and personal value. He and his father belonged to each other; their life was a shared life. Therefore, Jesus didn't suffer with insecurities or low self-esteem as we do because their perfect love removed all fear.

He was so in his father and his father was so in him that they were actually one, not two (John 5:23-24, 26; 8:16-18; 10:32; 14:9-11; 17:21). In fact, he was so close to his father that he was literally bi-located, with his father in heaven while on the earth, simultaneously, everyday – (John 3:13; 17:11-13). They were so close that Jesus spoke of himself and his father as "*we*" (John 3:11; 17:22). If you knew one, you knew the other; if you saw one, you saw the other; if you heard one, you heard the other (John 8:19; 12:44-45; 14:6-7). In fact, he was so united with his father, that he intuitively knew when others didn't know him (John 7:28-29; 8:54-55; 17:23). He was so united to Truth, Light, and Goodness, that he was able to discern error, darkness, and evil with pinpoint accuracy.

When Jesus told the multitudes not to worry about their lives, regarding food, drink or clothes, he spoke out of a personal familiarity with who his daddy really was to him (John 3:34-35; 16:15; 17:10). He knew his father loved him and them far more than the birds of the air and the lilies of the field (Matthew 6:25-31; 10:31; Luke 12:6-7, 22-32); he even went so far as to say to all the parents who were present, "*If you then, being evil, know how to give good gifts to your children, how much more will your father who is in heaven give good things to those who ask him!"* (Matthew 7:9-11, NKJV).

He knew his father loved him far more than the best parent in the world loves their children. I would even say that our father loved him far more than every parent who has ever lived in all of history has ever loved their children – and he loves you just the same.

This love is why Jesus was able to walk on water or sleep without fear in the back of the boat in the middle of the storm (Matthew 8:23-26; 14:22-32; Mark 4:35-41; 6:45-51). This love enabled him to stand toe-to-toe with violent crowds who wanted him dead. This is why he was who he was, lived the way he lived, and died the way he died.

He trusted his father so purely and distrusted himself so completely, in everything, that he transcended the realm of human explanation; he needed him more than oxygen, water, and food. He couldn't live without him. He needed his father who was his source, his life, his everything; this is why he said, *"Father, into your hands I commit my spirit"* before he breathed his last breath on the cross (Luke 23:46, NKJV). At the very moment when he was the weakest he would ever be, there was only one person he could think of to trust with his life; there was only one person he knew who really loved him (John 2:23-25; 19:10-11).

On one occasion, he spoke of himself as a vine and his father as a vinedresser, showing the weakness and vulnerability of his life in the hands of his daddy who cared for him so much that he actually knew the number of hairs on his head (John 15:1; Matthew 10:30). Though he was God, he never drew upon his nature as God to do anything. He lived out of his relationship with our Father, living in the very same manner that our Father desires to live with us. His whole life was lived as a human being, dependent upon the life and power of our Papa's world within him (John 3:2). He was the first to live like this, the first to completely hand over the entirety of his life to our Father, the first to truly believe him. It was only as he rested in their relationship that he could express our Father in any given situation.

His Integrity

"No man can purchase his virtue too dear, for it is the only thing whose value must ever increase with the price it has cost us. Our integrity is never worth so much as when we have parted with our all to keep it." – Ovid

In a day when integrity is rare or nearly extinct, we need to remind ourselves of what it means. The word *integrity* speaks of wholeness, honesty, uprightness, completeness, absoluteness, soundness, entirety, and stability; those who possess this virtue are honorable, uncorrupt, unbroken, unimpaired, undiminished, and undivided. Can you imagine a heart

> He was who he was, said what he said, and lived what he lived because it was right, not because it worked.

like this? What would it be like? Look like? Sound like? Do you know anyone like this? Fortunately, we have Jesus as our example.

He never blew in the wind or changed with the weather. He refused every voice and every influence around him that contradicted his true self, because he was entirely whole within himself. He was outwardly who he was inwardly in everything he said and did. He never wore one face to himself and another to everyone else so that he or anyone was confused as to which one was true. He never separated the life he lived from the words he spoke. His teachings were so entwined with his person that they lived beyond his natural life, because he spoke out of who he really was and always would be. He said and did nothing for which he would not be willingly responsible forever. He didn't need rules or laws; his changeless core was his law. Against all odds, against all instincts of self-preservation, he never compromised. In a time when truth was rare, he was true, even to his own hurt and eventual death.

He was who he was, said what he said, and lived what he lived because it was right, not because it worked. He knew when to say *"yes"* or *"no"* and never caved to outward pressure, public opinion, or brutal opposition; he knew his purpose and stayed the course. He didn't work to fit into other's expectations because he burned with the realization of who his father said he was. He never compromised himself and was willing, if need be, to lose every friend on earth in order to maintain his honor. He spoke the Truth, even when he knew it would produce conflict and division; he maintained his focus without any support from those closest to him. He behaved in ways that were in harmony with his personal values and made choices based on his relationship with his father, despite his relationship with everyone else.

He never compared himself to anyone or measured himself by others. Rather, he chose to be a first-rate version of himself and not be a second-rate version of someone else. He never allowed himself to become, in any way, like the systems he opposed while he was in them but lived to the beat of a different drummer, operating by a different set of values.

This was the essence of his success in life. This is how he was able to accomplish so much in such a short time. His unsullied character kept his focus strong, which, in turn, fueled his life.

Everything he said and did – his whole life – came out of who he was. He conducted himself temperately and restricted himself in all things according to his purpose; he did not run without a definite goal (1 Corinthians 9:24-27). His priorities were in order.

He kept first things first by loving his daddy and then loving people. This is why he fearlessly obeyed his father over and above men, because he feared and respected his father, not people, no matter who they were (Matthew 22:16; Luke 12:4-7).

Real Greatness

As Martin Luther said, Jesus *"conducted himself so humbly and associated with sinful men and women, and as a consequence was not held in great esteem,"* to such a degree that *"the devil overlooked him and did not recognize him. For the devil is farsighted; he looks for what is big and high and attaches himself to that; he does not look at that which is low down and beneath himself."*

Jesus was so secure in his father's love for him, that he did not love his life but rather hated it in order to keep it for eternity (John 12:23-25). He didn't care about preserving his life, ministry or reputation. He never used his power to benefit himself. His life was a living sacrifice to his father, conformed to the ways of heaven, not earth (Romans 12:1-2).

When his disciples informed him that someone, who was not in their group with them, was casting out demons in his name, he was not at all concerned (Mark 9:38; Luke 9:49-50). His ministry was a calling, not a career; he was a servant, not a card-carrying clergyman. He had nothing to protect, nothing to defend. *He* was not his ministry. He wasn't in competition with anyone at any time because he didn't have anything to lose that anyone could take from him. He wasn't insecure about having an outsider minister in his name without being ordained, approved or commissioned by him. He wasn't concerned about protecting his *"name brand"* because he never had a *"brand"* in the first place; nor was he worried about possibly being misrepresented by a complete stranger. So his answer to his disciple's dilemma was simple: *Leave them alone.*

And then, to take his selfless leadership to another level, he worked himself out of the job by equipping and releasing his disciples, the seventy, and so many others into Kingdom service (Matthew 10; Mark 6:7-13; Luke 9:1-6; 10:1, 17-20). He even shared the keys of the kingdom of heaven with Peter and never took them back when he displayed satanic behavior (Matthew 16:19). He didn't lose heart when his disciples exhibited stupidity, immaturity, and betrayal but rather empowered their fledgling lives and had the strength of character to see them through to the end because his trust was not in them.

Jesus didn't care about himself, his name, or his popularity; this is why he never carried a title, sought a position, or required preeminence. He never wore fancy garb or rode in regal carriages; rather, he dressed in common clothes and chose to ride donkeys over stallions. He appeared weak by human standards so that everyone could choose freely for themselves what to do with him.

In many ways, he was like one beggar telling another beggar where to find bread. His idea of greatness was childlikeness (Matthew 18:1-5; Luke 9:46-48) and sacrifice (Matthew 19:29). To him greatness was least-ness, not first-ness,; it was service, not hierarchy (Matthew 19:30; 20:20-28; Mark 9:33-37; 10:35-45; Luke 19:30; 20:20-28; 22:24-27; John 13:1-17). As he saw it, the best seat is reserved for those who take the lowest place (Luke 7:7-11).

And yet he said many things about himself that seemed arrogant and elitist to those who were adolescent, insecure, and weak in faith (See John 4:32, 34; 5:19-47; 7:37-38; 8:21-29, 38-59). Those who know who they are live who they are and are often perceived as being arrogant, but true humility is agreement with Truth. When Moses wrote about himself in Numbers 12:3 as the meekest man on the face of the earth, he wasn't lying or being conceited; he was simply agreeing with the Truth. When Jesus said things like *"Anyone who has seen me has seen the father"* or *"I and the father are one"* or *"My judgment is right"* or *"The Scriptures...testify about me,"* he was telling the Truth, even though most condemned him as a mad, demon-possessed liar. Jesus knew who he was and who he wasn't. He saw himself as his father saw him (John 5:31-32). Therefore, his kingdom identity was more real to him than his earthly counterpart.

Jesus knew he was the Christ, the Son of Man, the Son of God, the King of all kings, the "I AM," and so much more (Luke 22:66-23:3; John 9:35-37). He knew he was greater than Jonah and Solomon (Matthew 12:40-42; Luke 11:31-32). And yet he had the strength of character to stand, side by side, on level ground with the broken, sick, and tormented, restoring them to wholeness through the power of who he was in his father and their Kingdom (Luke 6:17-19). Jesus didn't have to be with *"somebodies," "big-wigs"* or *"movers-n-shakers,"* to feel good about himself. He didn't find his worth from being with *"bishops," "pastors," "popes," "apostles,"* or even *"super-apostles."* His reputation was one of a glutton and drunkard, a friend of *"nobodies,"* tax collectors, and sinners, and yet he was the *"the Bread of Life," "the Light of the world," "the Door of the sheep," "the Good Shepherd," "the Resurrection and the Life," "the Way, the Truth and the Life,"* and *"the True Vine"* (John 6:35, 41, 48, 51; 8:12; 9:5; 10:7, 9, 11, 14; 11:25; 14:6; 15:1, 5).

Unafraid To Be Me

There is nothing certain or secure in this world. Everything is temporal. And yet we often depend on things that are passing as if they will last forever. Why do we do this? Are we blind? Every human being, every natural system, every worldly ideal and philosophy will fail us sooner or later. And when it all begins to implode, how will we cope? How will we overcome in the midst of hell on earth? Will we determine the times, or will the times determine us? Will we lead or be led?

I was 16 when my parents divorced. I remember it as if it was yesterday. Seeing them split up after being so close to them for so long; after enjoying their friendship and the warm sunrays of their union together as "one flesh" with the Lord at the center of our family; after depending on the security of their love and shelter and peace, it all came crashing down. What I once trusted in to keep me safe and sound was gone forever.

As I think of all the relationships I've had in my life, all the betrayals, broken promises, and cold shoulders, I can't help but think that I would have made better decisions if I had known my true self and lived out of "him" instead of "the other guy." Every relationship drew on different parts of my heart and influenced me to be a little different with each person, but what if I had just been me the whole way through? Why did I cater to their whims? Why did I change for them?

> There has never been a time in history when being anyone other than who we were born to be was ever good for anyone.

For me, after enduring one identity crisis after another and failing everyone's expectations in one way or another, I am beginning to wake up to the one I've always been afraid to be. And now I am beginning to let the hell of uncertainty around me reduce me to the place where I see myself as he sees me. There is something about the pressures and tumult of life that are teaching me how to rest more and more in the peace that comes with being me, in him. He designed and built me to endure everything around me, and either I can let it beat me or I can let it bring out the best in me, leveling all my insecurities. He made me strong by making me like him and I am the only one who can kill his creation. And the same goes for you.

Most of us do not know who we are. We are like orphans and beggars without roots, without a home or family even though we may have a physical home and natural family. We live like God

28

is not our father; we live below our privileges as his children, wandering and squandering, blindly going about our days confused, empty, lonely, and discouraged. Sound familiar? Be honest!

Why do we judge ourselves and others by the style of our clothes or the size and look of our cars and houses? Why do we see ourselves and others in light of what we do rather than who we are? Why do we spend so much time busily consumed with things to do and people to see, running to and fro without a definite aim, with little to show for our toil? Are we not trying to compensate for something? Are we not trying to fill a void in our hearts?

We are human beings, not human doings. And yet we constantly judge each other by our gifts, our resumes, our ministries, our professions, our accomplishments and our qualifications. We are not what we have or what we do. Only *"paupers"* and *"beggars"* define themselves by their possessions or performance. We all play this same silly game day after day and no one ever really wins. Our only hope, the only way we can win, is to not play at all. It's all meaningless and only those who let their Father remind them of who they really are will live as they were designed to live. So let me ask you: How much of your activity and behavior is the result of your life in him? Do you live out of his life in you, or do you live out of yourself? Do you even know the difference?

I can't tell you how many times I've thought I was "nobody" simply because I was homeschooled or because I've always been a non-comformist or because I'm a "home body" who loves to read instead of getting dirty outside with everyone else or because I never went to college or because I've never felt like I "fit in." It's hard to think you're "some-body" when the pull of the crowd is so strong, trying to convince you that they are right and you are wrong. It's hard to impress people when meeting their standards is the only way they will ever really like you. But the truth is that there is nothing in this world that can ever really make me "somebody." If one day I feel I should get a degree in something, so be it, but that has nothing to do with who I am, and I should never find my identity in that or anything of a sort. The question is: Where does my trust lay? Do I really believe that my gift – who I am in him – will make room for me, or do I think I need to play by the rules of this world, and everyone in it, to excel? When people look down on me because I graduated from homeschool or because I don't go along to get along or because I've never taken one college course, should I care? Should I listen? Who made them a credible judge of who I was born to be? Who defines what's credible? What if we trusted Christ enough to follow his lead, despite the popular pull of "the professionals"? Is he not able to carry us?

Of course, I'm still learning to trust him this way. Though I want to follow him every day, there are times when I live as if he doesn't exist, as if I can take care of myself without his help. And while this may work for a time and even seem right on the surface, it never really ends well. But when I look at Jesus and how he lived, I see what enabled him to live the kind of life I've always been able to live, that's always been in him, in me. He lived free and full simply because he knew, firsthand, the length, breadth, height, and depth of our Father's love for him.

The times I've given into small thinking, which has always led to small living where I've lived below my privilege, are when I forgot who I am. As I once heard someone say, *"Pauperhood is relegated to the children of a lesser god."* To the degree that we see our Father as He really is, we will see ourselves as we really are and live the kind of life he's always meant for us. Then, we will no longer strive to earn his approval (or anyone else's) but will live, safe and secure, in the delight he has always had for us.

Those who know who they are live simply, purely, and effortlessly out of who they are, despite their surroundings or circumstances. They know that the perfect will of God is hidden in every moment, at every turn, no matter what they are doing, waiting for them to enjoy life every day from his perspective. They are not waiting for tomorrow or next year to be released from what they are doing now, so they can finally be used by God or finally be in his will. Rather, they are enjoying him every day as they partner with him in every area of life – in the home, on the job, at church, in the car and everywhere else – because everything is sacred to the Lord. To them, there is no such thing as *"secular"* and *"sacred,"* *"unspiritual"* and *"spiritual,"* because everything is holy to the Lord, and everything can become worship to God (i.e. washing the dishes, going to work, changing diapers, mowing the lawn, mentoring someone over coffee, cleaning the house, washing the clothes, etc.). For this brand of believer, everything they do every day is an opportunity to let God live and work through them, expressing his love in everything, reproducing the environment around them that they have cultivated within them.

As long as we live below our birthright as children of God, we will continue to misrepresent him to the world around us. Those who don't know who they are cannot be who God made them to be. Perception is reality. Clearly, the enemy has been successful in committing identity theft, killing us in so many ways without actually killing us, leaving us, for the most part, with a poverty-paradigm and slave-mentality which has led to pitiable living and behavior.

Sin is the result of living out of a mis-taken identity – an identity that is mis-taken – being who we were never created to be. But those who know who they are, in Christ, live very different lives. A true Christian is a *"little Christ."* When Jesus said, *"I am the Light of the world,"* and then said, *"You are the Light of the world,"* he was affirming us as those who are like him. Think about it: Is our *"Light"* from a different source than his? Is our *"Light"* less of a *"Light"* than his, or is it the same *"Light"* from the same source? When John wrote, *"As he is, so are we in this world,"* was he telling the Truth, or was he lying? Are we rotten, ragged sinners saved by grace, who are waiting for death or the *"rapture"* to take us to heaven? Or are we righteous, reigning saints who are sons and daughters of God Almighty bringing heaven, within us, into the earth, living his life every day? Are we just *"Christian soldiers"* of the faith, or are we heirs of God and joint heirs with Christ?

Have you ever wondered why Jesus taught us to pray, *"Our father"* rather than *"My father"*? Jesus didn't see himself as an only child but as the firstborn of many offspring (Acts 17:28; Romans 8:29; Colossians 1:15). Of course, when we say we are children of God, it is said so casually that it no longer has any real power or meaning. But what if we knew God as our Parent as much as our children know we are their parents? What if we related to him the way they relate to us? What if we felt as comfortable around him as they feel around us? What if we were as secure in his care for us as they are in ours? Our kids know that everything is "ours" – our food, our home, our cars, our everything - because we are a family. So they have nothing to fear; they can face anything knowing we are with them and for them and will never forsake them. They can be secure in knowing that there is nothing they can be, say, or do that will ever make us love them more or less. And yet Jesus said our love for our children – our flesh and blood – is wicked compared to our Papa's love for us. And we cannot pray enough, fast enough, worship enough, read the Bible enough, go to church enough or do anything enough to please him more than he already is. His love for us has nothing to do with our behavior. He loves "us" and even likes us...a lot!

> *"Let this mind be in you which was also in Christ Jesus"* (Philippians 2:5). What if we thought the way Jesus thinks?

Paul said, *"Let this mind be in you which was also in Christ Jesus."* (Philippians 2:5) What if we thought the way Jesus thought? Is it possible? If not, then why did Paul say this? Is Jesus our pattern or not? If he is then would we not live a richer, more wonderful life in him by allowing him to flush out of our minds every thought, feeling, and desire that disagrees with his thoughts, feelings, and desires? Consider this: The *word meditation is related to the word medicine. Therefore, when* we meditate on the life of Christ, we actually become more "healthy," through and through, in our spirit, soul, and body. This is what it means to repent, to re-think, or *"change the way we think."* Since we are who we think we are (Proverbs 23:7a), we cannot, as Bill Johnson says, afford to have any thoughts in our heads that are unlike his thoughts about us; otherwise, we'll never enjoy the kind of life he intended for us.

However, our love relationship with him is the foundation of our identity and is only possible for us as we abide in him who is love. He is Truth, and only he can make us free to be our true selves as we live in relationship with him. But this requires that we simply lean on him, or, as Jesus said, "abide in him" so that he can take over the responsibility of making us new from the inside.

When I started waking up to my true self – the person God created me to be all the time – I started losing the need to prove myself to everyone, to my parents, my in-laws, my wife and children, to friends and church leaders, and especially myself. I realized I had nothing to prove, that I simply needed to relax and be me. And now, every day, I'm learning, more and more, that it's useless to try and play the "performance-based approval" game; most people will only like me as long as I jump through all their hoops and keep jumping. So what's the use? The more I see myself the way Papa sees me, the bolder and freer I become. As my heart is flooded with the reality of who I am in his eyes, all the insecurities and fears I've struggled with all my life, (especially the fear of rejection) fall off like dead limbs on a tree.

So don't live another day in limbo like everyone else. Stop running from your destiny. Of course, this won't be easy, but it will be worth it. Be ready for opposition because almost everyone will fight against your choice, and they will not stop until they've won or you've endured past all their attempts at making you like them, bringing you down to their level. And don't be surprised if you lose friends, get kicked out of your church (or even many churches) or are snubbed by your whole family. You will be misunderstood, and people always fear what they don't understand. To the degree that you are free and secure within yourself, you will be shirked, and no matter what you do, they will never embrace you until you are like them or they are free like you.

There were times when I tried to fit in with my peers or everyone else by dressing like them or listening to their music or watching their movies or talking about what they liked or agreeing with their point of view or whatever but as I grew up and my heart was broken over and over again by those who rejected me the moment I didn't play their game, I began to realize that I wasn't born to please or be like anyone. I was born to follow him as he waters and tills the garden of my heart until I am who he made me to be. So stay the course, and when you are despised, forgive everyone who hurts you ("They know not what they do."). Whenever you face pain, praise, or persecution remember how Jesus behaved at such times and find solace in his life. Be content in being your Father's child. Relax and enjoy the person he made you to be. Those who really love you as you are will be few, but they will celebrate your life in him and be faithful to the end. Those who reject you may come back someday with a change of heart, and when that time comes, embrace them. Those who see your heart will learn from watching your life and will be inspired by the liberty you enjoy as you live "on earth, as it is in heaven."

- 2 -

An Unlikely Love

What if I told you that we have no idea what love is, that we've replaced it with everything it isn't and never was? What if we've believed every lie about the very thing that gives life to life? How can we believe that "It's all about love" and yet be so clueless about what it really is? Would that not taint everything else that we think and believe?

We've heard about the "goodness" and "kindness" of God over and over again. The problem is that we've allowed our culture and a partial, preferential view of the Gospels to define "goodness" and "kindness" for us. Of course, we *all* think we see Jesus clearly and, therefore, know what love is, but the truth is that we've been sold a bill of goods that shines light on half of who he was, leaving us with a distorted view of who he was and the life he wants for us in this world.

We've conveniently invented someone who we call Jesus and yet he has nothing to do with the genuine article. And what's sad is that if anyone of us ran into the same Jesus who was in Judea over two-thousand years ago, we'd run from him like our life depended on it. Why? Because the way he loved everyone doesn't fit "our" definition of love at all. But those who have the guts to start from scratch, with Jesus alone, will be changed forever.

Our Love

We all have different ideas of what love feels like, looks like, and sounds like based on how we've been conditioned by varying influences in our lives (e.g. parents, teachers, friends, ministers and books). Our definitions of love, which are constantly changing every day based on the impressions of everyday life, have made us into who we are today. As a result, we've developed a variety of grids or measurements regarding the essence and expressions of love whereby we judge everything and everyone as being loving or unloving, kind or unkind, friendly or unfriendly.

But do our perspectives agree with Christ's? Do our measurements measure up?

> Our love prefers unity over integrity, friendliness over honesty, sweetness over truth, acceptance over righteousness, and the approval of man over the approval of God.

Since we compare and measure ourselves and everyone else by ourselves and everyone else, we're nearly blind, especially when it comes to discerning the trueness of real love. Our love is simply not like Christ's because it can have a variety of related but distinct meanings in different contexts. Therefore, for the most part, it's earthly, conditional and appears sweet on the surface, in order to maintain appearances. Our love prefers unity over integrity, friendliness over honesty, sweetness over truth, acceptance over righteousness, and the approval of man over the approval of God. Our love is selfish while his love is self-less. Our love is motivated by what is best for us while his love is motivated by wisdom. Our love seeks short-term benefits while his love seeks our highest and best.

Instead of seeking true love, which is God, to know and experience him as he really is, we've created love in our own image and likeness and replaced him with a deity that is more like us than like him (of course, all of us would deny this). Instead of embracing his love, to search out the essence of his nature in Spirit and Truth, we've invented a fashionable love with many convenient sizes, shapes, and colors for everyone under the sun. As a result, we've all but lost God's love in the mix of a relativistic age where Truthful love is barely breathing.

Therefore, whenever the Lord has interacted with us, we've often misunderstood him when he's loved us his way. When he's corrected or disciplined us, we've taken it as rejection, not seeing his rod as love; when he's convicted us of sin, we've interpreted it as condemnation, guilt or shame, unknowingly stiff-arming his desire to make us like himself; when he's judged us, we've called it the work of the accuser, not seeing his mercy in his judgment; when he's brought us into the wilderness to mature us, we've taken it as punishment, unable to see his beauty in the desert; when he's spoken the Truth, we've rejected it when it wasn't communicated "in love" as "we" believe it should have been.

Jesus said the world would know we are his by our love, but whose love? Ours or his? The worlds or Heavens?

How did Jesus love people? How do we love people? And how do the two compare?

True Love

The true love of God is the *summum bonum*, the supreme good – greater than faith, hope, power, knowledge, and the law. And yet, it is weakened when mixed with even our greatest intentions because "Every man at his best state is altogether vanity." (Psalm 39:5, KJV)

We need a re-evaluation of real love as seen in the life of Jesus Christ. The Word became flesh and lived among us, but he didn't communicate like we do, and he didn't change his Word to be like ours, for our sake. He expressed the singular heart of God in

37

ways that were always good for us but rarely good to us from our limited, flea-sized point of view.

Jesus defines true love. Thus, everything we learn about love should be measured by him, by the life he lived, by the words he spoke and by the tone he took. Our tendency is to define love by first Corinthians thirteen ("The Love Chapter"), the epistles, good sermons, best-sellers and so many other things, especially when they confirm our ideals, but Jesus must be our plum-line and everything else must be compared to him. The Old Testament and Acts through Revelation have much to say about love, but they can only be truly understood through his life – not the other way around. Therefore, if what we believe about love does not agree with Jesus' life, we must be willing to dismantle everything we think we know about love and start from scratch with him at center-stage.

His ways are higher than our ways, and his thoughts are greater than our thoughts. There are depths and dimensions within God's love that surpass knowledge and extend far beyond our earthly love, that benefit eternity far more than our mere goodness ever could (Ephesians 3:18-19). We define love by the quality and quantity of what we think or don't think, say or don't say and do or don't do toward others, but 1st John 5:2-3 (Amp) is crystal clear:

"By this we come to know (recognize and understand) that we love the children of God: when we love God and obey his commands (orders, charges)--[when we keep his ordinances and are mindful of his precepts and his teaching]. For the [true] love of God is this: that we do his commands [keep his ordinances and are mindful of his precepts and teaching]…" (See also 2 John 6).

How do we know we love God and people? When we love God and obey him. This is the acid test.

But how do we know? By looking at Jesus who loved people by loving and obeying our Father (John 14:31; 1 John 2:5). He kept the first commandment first and kept the second commandment second and never confused the two (Mark 12:29-31). And while he loved people, he didn't trust them because he knew what was really in them (John 2:24-25). He was in the world but not of it, which is why he didn't love the world or the things in the world (1 John 2:15). His loyalties were unshakable. His devotion to our Father and their Kingdom was immovable.

He was consistent, a man of deep integrity, because he loved in deed and truth, not just in word (1 John 3:18). He always spoke the truth in love but not like we think, because when he spoke the truth, even in seemingly unkind ways, it was always for love's sake (Ephesians 4:15; John 5:19-47). Every word he spoke and everything he did communicated more love than anyone ever has since the beginning, but he didn't show it like we do.

> Religious tradition has manufactured a "Jesus" that is far more like us than our heavenly father.

His love was kind and severe, all the time, like the symmetrical love of a mother and father (Romans 11:22). He was a disciplinarian and a nurturer, a fighter and a lover, a master and a servant. His love was always redemptive and permeated his vision because he saw the potential in everyone around him which drove him to love them toward that potential even when it threatened their immediate comforts. There were times when his love was very offensive, but who did it offend?

Religious tradition has manufactured a "Jesus" that is far more like us than our heavenly father. We've envisioned someone who travelled around, telling people to be nice to each other, but how could this have gotten him killed? He wasn't safe or conventional. As Phillip Yancey wrote, "What government would execute Mister Rogers or Captain Kangaroo?" The tone and demeanor of his life rarely fit our common definitions of gentleness, kindness, humility, and self-control. His love was unlikely and, at times, unlovely as he was and is very unlike you and me.

The Rest of His Love

If Jesus were alive today, like he was in his first advent, he wouldn't fit any of our molds. He would be hated and rejected by most so-called Christians (including, perhaps, you and me). We would judge him through our tainted lenses, religious paradigms, and humanistic logic and label him by our own cultural nuances. And he would never survive as a so-called pastor or bishop, let alone an evangelist or teacher. He would be weighed and found wanting in comparison to today's average religious leaders who are rarely, if ever, rejected or slandered, let alone killed, as Jesus was.

As love personified, Jesus came with the baptism of the Holy Spirit and fire. With his winnowing fan in his hand, he thoroughly cleaned out his threshing floor, gathering and storing his wheat in his barn and burning up the chaff with unquenchable fire (Matthew 3:11-12; Luke 3:16-17). Can you imagine the success that would be had by your average minister today who brought these kinds of credentials to their job interviews? How many call-backs do you think they'd get?

Jesus didn't seek the approval or disapproval of men, because he wasn't interested in becoming a popular public figure (John 5:41, 44; 7:1-7). He never sought human praise or honor but was fully secure in his father's love; therefore, he could not be bribed or pressured with the affections of men and was thus free to be himself without fear (1 John 4:18). He never responded to human demands, out of human empathy or sympathy; he only did what he saw his father do and only spoke what he heard him say (John 5:17, 19, 30, 36; 6:38; 7:16-17; 8:16, 26, 28-29, 38, 40).

He was fully human but chose his father's disposition over human propensities. He didn't care like we care, because he didn't see as we see. He saw every situation from a higher perspective, enabling him to behave in a way that was best for everyone's ultimate good. His love was unconditional and self-less but upset many; it was illogical and eccentric but personified God's heart; it was contrary to the laws of human conscience but reflected heaven's way and the world hated him for it.

If we're going to truly see and know Jesus, as he really was (and still is, since he never changes), we must know both how he loved and how he didn't love. We also need to know what he loved and what he hated because you can tell what a person loves by what they hate. We have to know how he treated the meek, repentant, and broken versus how he handled those who "had it all together." He was patient and gentle (but not like us) toward the teachable and repentant, but he was very hard on the selfish and stubborn. He had integrity, taught the ways of God accurately, was indifferent to opinions and never pandered to his students (Matthew 22:16).

Jesus never consulted himself, taking counsel in his own soul as we so often do. He showed love heaven's way.

For example,

- When he healed the sick, diseased or handicapped, he used many crude and unusual methods that were very impolite, unusual and downright disgusting (i.e. Matthew 9:1-2; Mark 7:32-34; 8:22-26; John 4:46-49; 9:1-11). On the surface, his procedures seemed very offensive and even belittling, but from heaven's perspective love was always there.

- He healed the man who was crippled "with a deep-seated and lingering disorder for thirty-eight years" but didn't heal the "great number of sick folk" who were also present at the pool of Bethesda desperately needing a miracle (John 5:1-9, Amp). On the surface, it seems Jesus played favorites, but nothing could be further from the truth (Romans 2:11; Ephesians 6:9). As for why Jesus healed only one out of a multitude, I'm not quite sure and don't expect to understand everything that was going through his head at the time; he could have easily shown great love by healing everyone who was there but he did not allow himself to be led by sympathetic feelings roused by the spectacle of misery. Besides, love is just as often in the withholding as in the giving of healing depending on the leading of our father who "knows best."

- When he was informed that Lazarus, his dear friend, was sick, he didn't immediately go to help him. Rather, he waited four days and then went to him after he had already died (John 11:1-44). Of course, when he got there, he raised him from the dead. But why didn't Jesus go to see his friend the moment he heard he was sick? Why did he deliberately let Lazarus die and his family grieve? Did he not love them? Of course! But the reason he let Lazarus die was so that he could show his glory by raising him from the dead. Obviously, Jesus' eternal purpose, as set by his father, in letting Lazarus die before he raised him from the dead, was more important than healing him while he was sick. Depending on your perspective, you may call this insanity or genius but doesn't all genius have a touch of madness?

- He spoke in parables and fuzzy-language to the multitudes, religious and political leaders and even to his very own followers and often expressed frustration when they didn't understand what he was saying (Matthew 15:17; 16:9,10; Mark 4:13; 6:52; 8:17-21; Luke 9:45; John 3:9-10; 6:22-71; 8:43). He didn't use the latest and greatest principles of public speaking in order to reach his audiences, to appeal to their way of learning. If he had been considerate of his hearers, by our standards, he would have "known his audience" and done his best to communicate in a way that was simple and down-to-earth for them, no matter who they were. Right?

- He saw into people's secret lives – into their hearts – and often disclosed them, removing their ability to hide from the Truth (Matthew 9:4-6; 12:25-37; John 1:48; 2:24-25; 4:16-19). He didn't coddle the darkness but exposed it, which brought embarrassment to the proud and self-righteous who kept their skeletons, demons, and blemishes in the closets of their hearts.

- He publically rebuked, condemned, and judged individuals, crowds, and cities for their silliness, stupidity, and stubbornness, for witnessing his miracles without turning from their sins toward God (Matthew 11:20-24; Luke 10: 13-15; 11:27-32). He called his generation evil, hypocritical, irresponsible, and adulterous (Luke 11:29; 12:54-59). Does that sound like love to you? No! But he rebuked (and still rebukes) those he loves (Hebrews 12:5-11).

One time, after healing someone, he gave them a strong warning, "See, you are well! Stop sinning or something worse may happen to you" (John 5:14, Amp). Was that a threat? Of course not, but it sure sounded like it, didn't it? And it didn't seem very encouraging at all either. But why do we put so much stock into how things "sound" and "seem"? Why are we so quick to think the worst? Why do we have to immediately jump to the "glass-is-half-empty" point of view? The truth is that Jesus wanted them to stay whole and gave the no-nonsense tip for how to keep the life they had been given.

- He said many harsh things to the multitudes for their dullness, rebellion, wickedness and unbelief (Matthew 16:27; 17:14-20; John 6; 7:7, 19; 9:39). There were also times that he came across as bossy, elitist, cocky, and cold-hearted (John 7:16-17, 24, 28-29, 34, 37-38; 8:12, 14-59). By normal standards, he wasn't encouraging or seeker-sensitive as a leader, nor was he comforting to those who doubted him. In fact, there were times when he openly threatened people with death if they would not repent, saying, ."..Unless you repent...you will all likewise perish and be lost eternally," like the Galileans who were slaughtered by Pilate and the eighteen people who were crushed to death by the tower that fell in Siloam (Luke 13:1-5, Amp). Clearly, he didn't preach or teach the party line, ebbing-n-flowing with "ministry trends" for mass appeal or cultural relevancy. As a result, he often fell behind in "the polls."

- He entered the Temple, on at least one occasion, and violently drove out the merchants and their customers. He pushed over their money-tables and overturned the stalls of those who were selling doves, yelling at them, saying, "The Scriptures declare, 'My Temple will be called a place of prayer,' but you have turned it into a den of thieves!" (Matthew 21:12-13; Mark 11:15-18; Luke 19:45-48; John 2:13-22). His father's zeal burned in him like a bonfire. This was a major expression of divine love and respect for his father, despite the way it looked or what everyone may have thought at the time because he loved and respected his father more than he loved and respected anyone else (Hebrews 12:5-11).

- He wept over Jerusalem, broken over its rejection of his embrace. As a result, he pronounced desolation upon her house and the removal of his presence and said, "You will not see me again until you say, Blessed...is he who comes in the name of the Lord" (Matthew 23:37-39, Amp).

- He cursed an unfruitful fig tree for being unfruitful even though it wasn't the season for figs (Matthew 21:18-22; Mark 11:12-14, 22-24). Why would he curse an innocent organism that was obviously doing what it was supposed to do? He did it as a prophetic picture of what he was about to do to Israel (which is typified, in Scripture, as a fig tree) and to teach his disciples about faith.

- He raised and maintained the standard, value and integrity of the Kingdom (Matthew 5-7; 20:20-22; Luke 9:23-26). He never twisted or broadened the straight and narrow for mercy's sake (Matthew 7:13-14; Luke 13:22-30). He never lowered the bar or compromised the price of authentic discipleship; in fact, he made "the cost" too great for some to bear (Matthew 10:34-39; Luke 14:25-33; John 8:31).

  He never made it easy to follow him. As a result, he separated the curious from the committed (See Matthew 8:18-22; 19:16-26; Mark 10:17-27; Luke 9:57-62; 18:18-23; John 6:22-71). He did not bring peace but division (Matthew 10:34-39; Luke 12:51-53; 14:26-27). His evangelistic style and methodology were often very hard, cold, and unpopular compared to most well-intentioned evangelists today. For instance, in John 5:19-47, Jesus gave a face-slapping message and finished by saying, "I simply mention all these things in order that you may be saved." Today, we would tell Jesus that if he really cared about "saving souls," he be more gentle, caring and compassionate; if he really loved the lost, he would tone it down to meet the people where they are instead of beating them with an abusive message.

- When his disciples – his inner circle of "faithful" followers – displayed unbelief and stupidity, he didn't coddle them or encourage them that they would eventually "get it." Rather, he scolded them and, at times, would be very harsh, saying things like, ."..Are you...yet dull and ignorant [without understanding and unable to put things together]?...Oh you of little faith, why do you doubt?...Why are you so timid and fearful? How is it that you have no faith (no firmly relying trust)?...Do you not yet discern or understand? Are your hearts in [a settled state of] hardness?...O foolish ones [sluggish in mind, dull of perception] and slow of heart to believe (adhere to and trust in and rely on) everything that the prophets have spoken!" (See Matthew 8:23-26; 14:28-31; 15:15-16; 16:5-12; Mark 4:40; 8:13-21; Luke 8:22-25; 24:25; John 14:8-9; 20:26-29; 21:15-23, Amp). Jesus even went so far as to ask his disciples if they were as dense as the Pharisees (Matthew 15:1-16). And get this: Jesus didn't open his disciple's minds to understand the Scriptures until the end of his ministry (Luke 24:45). How considerate was that?

And to further illustrate his charm as a mentor, he once called Peter "Satan" when he saw things from a human point of view rather than God's (Matthew 16:21-25). Then, on another occasion, he called Judas a devil (John 6:70-71). Does this sound like someone who was full of love? Of course not! Did Jesus love his disciples? Of course, which is why he treated them the way he did. How would you like to be discipled by someone like this?

• As for the Pharisees, Sadducees, Scribes, Lawyers, and Teachers of the Law, we know Jesus loved them very much, as he loved everyone; in fact, he loved them so much that he spoke the Truth to them, in love, even to the degree that he scolded and shamed them to their faces, time and time again, verbally undressing them in front of everyone. His language and tone was always very strong and often insulting, leaving the "leaders" shell-shocked and embarrassed (Matthew 9:3-7; 12:1-14, 24-45; 15:1-14; 16:1-4; 19:1-12; 21:23-45; 22:15-46; 23:1-36; Mark 2:23-28; 3:1-6; 7:1-13; 10:1-12; 12:1-40; Luke 5:27-39; 6:1-11; 11:37-54; 13:14-17; 14:1-6; John 9:39-41; 10:24-

26; Hebrews 12:5-11). Of course, his contention wasn't with flesh and blood men but against dark rulers, authorities, and powers in the heavenly realms (Ephesians 6:12). And yet he engaged the religious leaders who, knowingly or unknowingly, enabled and embodied the greatest religious evils of his time. In fact, he oftentimes appeared to have a personal vendetta against the religious and political leaders, though it was never personal (Luke 13:31-33). From the common-man's perspective, it looked like Jesus had no patience for these leaders who were blind and deceived and, therefore, didn't know any better. He didn't "Kill them with kindness" or "Love them into change" as we would think, and yet he loved them more than anyone else ever had and ever would.

- When the Syrophoenician woman came to Jesus begging that he would deliver her daughter of a tormenting demon, he responded, "I was sent only to the lost sheep of the house of Israel." But this didn't stop her. She threw herself at his feet and worshipped him, pleading all the more for help, to which he said, "It is not right...to take the children's bread and throw it to the little dogs." Did you catch that? "Sweet and gentle Jesus" called this woman a "dog"! Does this sound like the Jesus our Sunday-School teacher told us about? Where was the love in that? On the surface, it looks like Jesus didn't care anything about her or her daughter when, in fact, he did love her and was simply testing her character and the strength and persistence of her faith. He was "rude" in order to test her true nature, to see if she would allow herself to become offended or embittered. Besides, those who know the story, know that she passed the test by her right-response; she did not allow her feelings to be hurt and, in the end, received her restored daughter (See Matthew 15:22-28 and Mark 7:24-30).

- One time, when Jesus was speaking to a crowd, someone told him that his mother and brothers were waiting to speak with him. To this he said, "Who is my mother, and who are my brothers?" Then he pointed to his disciples and said, "Here are by mother and my brothers. For whoever does the will of my father in heaven is my brother and sister and mother!" (Matthew 12:46-50, Amp) Can you imagine what this looked and sounded like to everyone who was there? Can you think of how this may have hurt Mary and his blood brothers? Was he disowning his family, or was he just trying to shock everyone? No! He was speaking out of his priorities, his Kingdom perspective, putting his spiritual family before his biological family. He didn't show favoritism to anyone but put everyone on a level playing field, putting conditions on those who wished to be his true family.

> Most were uncomfortable with him because he was simply true – not everyone wanted a real friend and, sadly, most still don't.

What if someone – anyone – actually loved like this today? Would we like them? How popular would they be, in the church, in the highways and byways, in the marketplace? How many parties would they be invited to? How many true friends would they have? How would we treat them? Would we be their friend? How would we talk about them? Would we invite them over for dinner? Would we let them into our hearts?

Think about it – seriously!

He modeled real friendship. He didn't flatter, lie, compromise, or pretend in any way in order to "win friends and influence people." He didn't wear masks, flaunt himself or his abilities, serve out of self-interest or say one thing and do another. He was loyal, generous, honest, fair, and self-less when everyone around him was not, in one way or another. Most were uncomfortable with him because he was simply true – not everyone wanted a real friend and, sadly, most still don't.

Your Real Nature

Jesus told us to love each other as he loves us and later told us that everyone would know we are his by our love (John 13:34-35). But, as we've seen, his love is not at all like ours, and it is the kind and quality of our love that determines who we are following. We will live the love we've learned. The question is: Who was our teacher? The World? Your Pastor? Your Church? Tradition? The Media? Your parents? A friend? Who?

When Jesus commanded his disciples and, in turn, commanded us to love each other in the same way that he loves us, he was, at the same time, directing us away from our love, away from the love of the world and every other kind of love that was and is not like his (John 15:12). But this requires a choice.

What if we actually loved like Jesus? What would that look like, sound like or feel like? What if we stopped comparing ourselves to each other? What if we stopped measuring each other by each other? What if we adopted the only love that can ever advance the Kingdom?

What if we stopped doing "the right thing," being "a good person," and chose, instead, to follow the only One who is right and good? What if we stopped focusing on being "kind" or "hard," "merciful" or "tough," and just relaxed in being who he wants us to be every moment? What if we stopped letting our hearts be leveraged by the way we were loved in the past by our parents, friends or extended family? What if we weren't influenced by our environment or the people around us but simply lived out of who we are in him? Would we not influence everything and everyone around us for good 24/7?

Do we want to be relevant to this world or to the Kingdom of God? Who do we want to have the most in common with, people or Christ? Our great aim should be to follow our father's example, to know him, see him, hear him, and follow his lead in everything we do, out of love for him. If Jesus did nothing independently, of his own authority, speaking and acting out of his own mind, but reflected his father's words and actions of love in everything he said and did, how much more should we commit ourselves to obeying our father in everything we say and do?

The nature and demeanor of Christ is already in you because you came from him and he is in you. So let it flow through you and don't be afraid when it comes to the surface in a form and tone you don't understand or agree with. If you love like the world loves while trying to live the Christian life, are you really a Christian at all? How can we pander to one and give lip service to the other?

Those who truly know this love - his love - will be filled with all the fullness of God, "wholly filled and flooded with God himself" (Ephesians 3:19). Christ in them will become Christ on them as he lives and loves through them. They will not be governed or controlled by the world and its systems or the people and things in it; nor will they be manipulated by what "seems" best or "appears" right. They will only be governed and controlled by the love of Jesus who fills them, because his love never fails.

- 3 -

Like Father, Like Sons

Years ago I read a little book called *Jesus, the Pattern Son*, by Bill Britton, which in many ways started me on this fanatical journey into Jesus Christ. Since that time, seeing Jesus as the only true "pattern" for all that he is doing in me, in his people, and in this world has changed the way I think about every area of my life. There are so many "voices" that we have allowed to speak into our lives, and the sad thing is that we have in many ways given them a platform right beside Christ, in our hearts, to influence our choices. Some of these "voices" are standing in front of him, drowning him out entirely, while other "voices" are standing slightly behind him, just over his shoulder, poking their heads in every once in awhile to put in their two-cents while he is trying to talk to us.

Jesus was "our Father's son" and still is, but we often behave like we have a different daddy or even many daddies who fill our heads and hearts with all kinds of nonsense, which the world calls "good advice." We go to the doctor, to the pastor, to our spouse, to a friend, or to our parents *before* we've given our Father a chance to tell us what He thinks and feels about our situation. As Joyce Meyer once said, "We pick up the phone before we go to the throne." Why is that? Do we not know who we are and who our Daddy is? Do we not know how much He loves us? Why do we not honor Him? Is there anyone wiser than Him? Are we "too cool" to need Him? Are we "beyond" Him?

Ask yourself: Who do you look up to? Who do you want to be like? Who is your idol? Who do you go to for "good advice" or "wise counsel"? Who is your standard? Can we continue to call ourselves Christians while we have so many "gods" in our lives that are blurring or entirely blocking the Lord from our eyes?

51

Ephesians 4:13 speaks of a people who will "...[...arrive] at really mature manhood (the completeness of personality which is nothing less than the standard height of Christ's own perfection), the measure of the stature of the fullness of the Christ and the completeness found in Him." (Amp) But this "measure" cannot exist where there is a mixture.

When God told Moses to build the tabernacle after the pattern of the tabernacle in Heaven, it was done as a prophetic type of the Word who later became a human being named Jesus and reflected our Father in this world (Exodus 25:40; John 1:14, 18; Luke 10:22; Colossians 1:15; 2:9; Hebrews 1:3; 8:5). As our Father lived, he lived. As our Father spoke, he spoke. As our Father worked, he worked. And when he made a judgment-call, he was always right because he never chose his own will. He had no desire to meet his own needs but sought only his Father's pleasure (John 5:30). This is why anyone who saw and knew Jesus saw and knew our Father as well (John 1:18; 8:19b; 12:45; 13:20b; 14:7-11; 15:23-24; 17:4, 6).

There are many who do not believe this kind of life is possible. But, as someone once said, "The Christian life isn't hard, it's impossible," which is why Christ is the only one who can help us; he is the only one who has the power to make us just like himself. And yet, I am the only one who can keep Him from transforming me by reducing me to the simplicity of Christ, that is in Christ (no one else is responsible for my choices). I am the only one who has the power to promote or prevent His work in my life. The true Christian life is not for the faint of heart but for those who are willing to run boldly into their own demise, into the end of themselves, into Christ.

Jesus' life defines what Watchman Nee called "the normal Christian life." Everything about him reflected our Father and reflects the kind of life we were born to live. Are we ready to be like our Father too? How about you?

His Words

Every word Jesus spoke was not his own, but his Father's. How do we know this? Because he said, "He Who sent Me is true (reliable), and I tell the world [only] the things that I have heard from Him...I tell the things which I have seen and learned at My Father's side...I have never spoken on My own authority or of My own accord or as self-appointed, but the Father Who sent Me has Himself given Me orders [concerning] what to say and what to tell. And I know that His commandment is (means) eternal life. So whatever I speak, I am saying [exactly] what My Father has told Me to say and in accordance with His instructions...What I am telling you I do not say on My own authority and of My own accord." (John 8:26, 38; 12:49-50; 14:10, Amp. See also John 7:16; 8:28)

> The true Christian life is not for the faint of heart but for those who are willing to run boldly into their own demise, into the end of themselves, into Christ.

When people asked him questions, he didn't give "pat-answers" off the top of his head; nor did he rely on the religious training he received as a boy. And yet, he spoke like one who had learning far beyond his years. Of course, this mystified the religious leaders of his day who said, "How is it that this Man has learning [is so versed in the sacred Scriptures and in theology] when He has never studied?" (John 7:15, Amp)

When Jesus finished his Sermon on the Mount "the crowds were astonished and overwhelmed with bewildered wonder at His teaching, for He was teaching as one Who had [and was] authority, and not as [did] the scribes." (Matthew 7:28-29, Amp) They were amazed and at times terrified, saying, "What is this? What new (fresh) teaching!" (Mark 1:27, Amp); while, at other times, they said his teachings were "too tough to swallow." (John 6:60, Message) But, in general, "they were amazed...for His word was with authority and ability and weight and power." (Luke 4:32, Amp)

What Jesus heard "in the dark...in the ear" he spoke "in the light...on the housetops" (Matthew 10:27). He spoke mysteries in mysterious ways, and only those who loved and desired God's will could discern for themselves whether his teachings were from God or from himself (Matthew 13:34-35; Mark 4:2, 33; John 7:17). So when he was misunderstood, which happened all the time, he didn't take it personally because he knew his words weren't for everyone (John 8:43). In the end, his only responsibility was to give what he was given, despite the results (John 14:24).

His Works

Every action Jesus took was not his own, but his Father's, for he said, "The Son is able to do nothing of Himself (of His own accord); but He is able to do only what He sees the Father doing, for whatever the Father does is what the Son does in the same way [in His turn]...I am able to do nothing from Myself [independently, of My own accord--but only as I am taught by God and as I get His orders]...I do nothing of Myself (of My own accord or on My own authority)...He Who sent Me is ever with Me; My Father has not left Me alone, for I always do what pleases Him...the Father Who lives continually in Me does...(His) works (His own miracles, deeds of power)...I do as the Father has commanded Me, so that the world may know (be convinced) that I love the Father and that I do only what the Father has instructed Me to do. [I act in full agreement with His orders]." (John 5:19, 30; 8:28, 29; 14:10, 31, Amp)

For Jesus to live like this, he had to be aware of what our Father was doing, which he admitted when he said, "We must work the works of Him Who sent Me and be busy with His business while it is daylight; night is coming on when no man can work." (John 9:4, Amp) What did he mean by this? Well, if "light" in the Scriptures often speaks of understanding or enlightenment, and "night" refers to darkness which often speaks of disorientation or confusion, then he was saying, "We must do what our Father is doing while we can see what He is doing because there will be times when we will be 'in the dark'."

Jesus walked in the light – that is, he walked when he could see – which is why he never stumbled (John 11:9-10). He never "did his own thing" or made things up "as he went," because he never left room for creative or poetic license or an independent thought. He didn't allow men to steer his decisions, and he certainly didn't care about maintaining cultural relevance or being PC (politically correct).

He Struggled Too

Of course, just like us, Jesus had times, as in Gethsemane, when he wrestled with rebellion, between doing his will or his Father's. His soul – his mind, emotions, and will – was filled with sorrow, grief, and severe mental and physical anguish, so much so that his skin perspired great drops of blood on the ground as he prayed, "My Father, if it is possible, let this cup pass away from Me; nevertheless, not what I will [not what I desire], but as You will and desire." And he didn't pray this once but three times, enduring severe pressure as he fought to submit his "will and desire" to his Father's (See Matthew 26:36-44; Mark 14:32-41; Luke 22:39-46; Amp).

Jesus wasn't a machine that involuntarily obeyed its programming. Instead, he was a person like you and me who had the freedom to disobey at any time during his life. And yet he developed such a love for our Father that he said, "My food (nourishment) is to do the will (pleasure) of Him Who sent Me and to accomplish and completely finish His work...I do not seek or consult My own will [I have no desire to do what is pleasing to Myself, My own aim, My own purpose] but only the will and pleasure of the Father Who sent Me...I do nothing of Myself (of My own accord or on My own authority)." (John 4:34; 5:30; 8:28. Amp)

I like the way the Message Bible paraphrases these verses: "The food that keeps me going is that I do the will of the One who sent me, finishing the work he started...I can't do a solitary thing on my own: I listen, then I decide...I'm not out to get my own way but only to carry out orders...I'm not making this up, but speaking only what the Father taught me." [See also Job 23:12; John 4:32; 6:38]

Roots & Fruits

Jesus said to his disciples, "I am the True Vine...My Father is the Vinedresser...you are the branches." (John 15:1, 5b, Amp) By saying this, he was linking his need for our Father with our need for him and our Father, revealing the culture of trust and dependence that has always existed within the Godhead. Of course, we often think Jesus was self-sufficient because he was God, but this simply isn't true as all the Scriptures we've covered in this chapter so far have shown. Besides, a vine needs a vinedresser, *just like* the branches; both *need* a gardener to take care of them. Jesus wasn't able to do anything "independently" because he loved our Father's will more than anyone else's (see John 5:19, 30; 8:28, 29; 14:10, 31, Amp). Sure, he could have done many "good things" on his own without our Father, as we so often do today, and he could have met everyone's approval in the process, but he knew he had to depend on his Father 100% in order to fulfill his Kingdom assignment.

According to Philippians 2:5-8, Jesus stripped himself of his deity and became a flesh and blood human being, just like you and me. He laid down his omniscience (unlimited knowledge), omnipotence (unlimited power), and omnipresence (unlimited ability to be everywhere at once). Therefore, he didn't say or do anything as God but rather lived his whole natural life out of the overflow of his relationship with our Father, fully yielded and dependent on Him for everything, everyday (John 3:2; 10:32). This is where his strength and confidence came from. This is why he was such a fruitful vine.

Like any good son who looks up to his dad, Jesus looked up to our Father and followed his lead. Doing his Father's will and hearing every word that proceeded from His mouth was his bread-and-butter (John 4:34; Matthew 4:4). If he had a "methodology" or "formula," per se, for his life and ministry, it had to be that of simple, utter dependence on our Father with one possible, practical motto: *pray*, *hear*, *obey*...period!

> Jesus didn't say or do anything as God but rather lived his whole natural life out of the overflow of his relationship with our Father, fully yielded and dependent on Him for everything, everyday.

This explains why the Dove of the Holy Spirit landed on Jesus at the Jordan River and never flew away (John 1:32-33). He lived every day, with the presence of the Dove in mind, ever sensitive to his needs. He lived carefully, faithfully, and obediently toward our Father, "timidly shrinking from whatever might offend God." (Philippians 2:12, Amp; Hebrews 5:7, Amp) [For more on this, read The Sensitivity of the Spirit by R.T. Kendall]

When Jesus was questioned by the Jews about where he came from and who his Father was, he said, "...I come from His [very] presence." (John 7:29, Amp) In other words, "I am from Him," (KJV) or literally, "I exist from Him." This not only means that Jesus came from his Father as a child comes from a parent or water comes from a well, but that he also lived out of and existed from our Father in the same way a house is powered by electricity or a plant is strengthened by the sun. This was his way of life, his "root-system."

And when Jesus said, "...I come from His [very] presence," he didn't say, "I came from His presence," as if he left his Father to "come to earth," hoping to return to his Father at a later date. Instead, he lived, moment by moment, "from" or out of his Father's presence and gave to the world what he received from that place. And whenever he climbed a mountain to pray, he ascended in more ways than one, through personal interaction with our Father, so that when he descended the mountain, he, in a sense, re-entered the natural realm with fresh manna from Heaven for those in need. Then, when he had given what he had, he returned to the Secret Place, which could be done at *any* time to re-charge and re-tool for his next assignment.

Jesus lived with his Father and never left (John 8:38). This is why he said to the guards who were sent to arrest him, ."..Where I *am* you cannot come." (John 7:34, KJV) Then again, while conversing with Nicodemus, he said, "No one has ever gone up to heaven, but there is one Who *has* come down from heaven--the Son of Man [Himself] Who *is* (*dwells*, *has* His home) in heaven." (John 3:13, Amp) So, when he was with the guards, he was somewhere they couldn't come even though they were in his physical presence. Then, when he was chatting with "Nick," he was in heaven even though he had already "come down from heaven."

How did he do that? Well, in Luke 17:21, Jesus said, "Behold, the kingdom of God is within you [in your hearts] and among you [surrounding you]." (Amp) This is how Jesus lived in Heaven, while on the earth. He lived in the world while a greater World was in him. He did "come down from heaven" because heaven is in a "higher" dimension of life and yet he also lived in heaven because heaven was in him and he was in our Father.

On one occasion, in John 17, Jesus seemed to transcend his natural environment while spending time with his Father in prayer for his disciples. We know this because in verse 11 he prayed, "And *now* I am no more in the world but these *are* in the world, and I *come* to thee..." (KJV) Then, in verses 12 and 13, he prayed, "While I *was* with them in the world, I kept them in thy name...And *now* come I to thee." (KJV) Jesus was in the world but not of it (John 17:16, 18). He lived in Heaven and on earth at the same time by walking with our Father every day. [Read Brother Lawrence's book called *Practicing the Presence of God* to see how one friend of God experienced this kind of life for himself.]

> If you are "born from above," then God is your Father, Jesus is your big brother, and you have everything you need – by the Spirit – to follow him as he followed our Father.

Jesus lived in our Father and our Father lived in him, so much so that the Father did His works through his son (John 14:10-11; Acts 2:22). However, if Jesus hadn't given himself fully to this union, which he always had a choice to do (as do we), he would not have been able to live so fruitfully the way he did.

But what motivated Jesus to live like this? Well, in John 14:31, Jesus said, ."..I do as the Father has commanded Me, *so that* the world may know (be convinced) that I love the Father..." (Amp) Jesus obeyed His Father and refused his own way (Proverbs 14:12) for one reason: because He loved Him. This was his incentive, his source of inspiration, his reason for living. He laid down his will, sacrificed his life and gave everything away for love, and now he is calling us to follow his lead.

How Should We Then Live?

If you are "born from above," then God is your Father, Jesus is your big brother, and you have everything you need – by the

Spirit – to follow him as he followed our Father (John 1:14, 17; 3:6; 1 Corinthians 1:4; 5:10; 2 Corinthians 9:8). The blood of our Father, His essence, His DNA, is in Jesus and us, because we are His children, His offspring and are, therefore, His heirs and co-heirs with Jesus (2 Peter 1:4; Romans 8:15-17).

"Out of His fullness (abundance) we have all received [all had a share and we were all supplied with] one grace after another and spiritual blessing upon spiritual blessing and even favor upon favor and gift [heaped] upon gift." (John 1:16, Amp)

We can receive nothing except as it has been given to us from Heaven and we've received "His fullness," His abundance, "His unspeakable gift" (2 Corinthians 9:14) and "the unsearchable riches of Christ" (Ephesians 3:8). As John the Baptist said, ."..Don't think he rations out the Spirit in bits and pieces. The Father loves the Son extravagantly. He turned everything over to him so he could give it away — a lavish distribution of gifts. That is why whoever accepts and trusts the Son gets in on everything, life complete and forever!" (John 3:34-36, Message). This is a loaded promise. Everything that belongs to our Father belongs to Jesus, and everything that belongs to Jesus belongs to our Father, and we have been grafted into Them (John 13:3; 17:10, 21, 22).

But how can this be? Because Jesus is in our Father and we are in him and he is in us (John 14:20). Think about that very carefully. Let it sink in. Can you imagine anything more wonderful than that? What if we actually believed this? How different would our lives be?

Remember, Jesus is the Vine, and we are his branches (John 15:1-6). His life, his sap, his blood, is flowing through us even now if we are intimately joined to him. And if we stay yielded to our Daddy, surrendered in His hand, He will use us to show Himself to the world speaking His words through our lips and living His life through our bodies.

As Jesus followed and reflected our Father, so we must wake up to who we are, to follow and reflect him as well, walking in the Light as he is in the Light (John 8:12; 17:10; Galatians 1:15-16; 1 John 1:7). As the Father sent Jesus, Jesus is also now sending us (John 17:18; 20:21). As the Father loved the world through His Son, He wants to continue to show the power and purity of His love through us (John 13:34). Everything Jesus meant for his disciples, he means for us who follow him wherever he goes (John 17:20). As the Father was in the Son and the Son was in the Father, They have called us to be one with Them so the world will believe. Jesus has given us the glory he received from his Father to make us one even as they are one (John 17:22). He is in us and our Father is in him, and as the Father loves his firstborn Son, He, in the same way, loves us and has freely given us all things (Matthew 11:27; 19:26; 21:22; John 3:35; 14:26; 15:15; 15:15; 17:23; Romans 8:32).

Everything Jesus did was meant to show us our Father, so that the love he received from his Father would be in us and he would be in us (John 17:26). And now the world – and the church, whether they know it or not – is waiting for those who will believe Christ and live His life out loud, reflecting Him in everything they say and do every day (Romans 8:19).

Jesus hung his credibility as God's son upon his Father's works worked through him (John 5:36; 10:25, 37-38). So, think about it: should the world believe we belong to the Lord and that He has sent us if we do not do His works? No! And yet, Jesus himself said we would do the things he did and even "greater works." (John 14:12) And now he lives within us, by his Spirit, along with his Father and all the divine fullness of their Kingdom to aid us in the fulfillment of this promise (See Matthew 28:30; Luke 17:20-21; John 14:16-18, 23, 26; 16:7, 13; Acts 17:27-28; Romans 8:15-19; 1 Corinthians 3:16-17; 6:19-20; 2 Corinthians 6:14-18; 13:5; Galatians 4:6-7; Ephesians 2:19-22; 3:17, 19; Colossians 1:19, 26-27; 1 John 4:4). So, how can we say we don't "have what it takes"? How can we say we aren't ready or able? How long can we continue to blame our inadequacies or make excuses? He who is in us is greater than all our flaws, faults, and failings. The only question is: where does our faith rest? In his power or our weakness, in his wisdom or ours, in his Truth or what we think?

Discovering who Jesus is, what he is like, being changed into his likeness and living like him out of the overflow of our intimacy with him, is the great journey of every true believer. It is time for the love and power of the Father to invade this world through yielded believers who are as He is, for love's sake (1 John 4:17).

So follow him. Live like he lived. Pray like he prayed. Hear like he heard. Obey like he obeyed. Study his life. Devour the four Gospels. Let the Holy Spirit show you who Jesus really is and who you really are because of who he is and what he's done. Jesus wants you to be with him where he is, so that you can see his glory and goodness, which surpasses your highest hopes and dreams (John 12:26; 17:24). Then, when you see him, you will be changed by him and you will never settle for anything less ever again.

- 4 -

When Jesus Comes Over For Dinner

The table used to speak of friendship, fellowship, and intimacy; it used to be the place of openness and transparency, of sharing and being shared. Today, we are too busy to sit down and enjoy one another over a home-cooked meal where open hearts and vulnerable lives come together. It is so much easier to hide behind TV, computers, or other things and activities than it is to be together and enjoy each other, as family.

When Jesus reclined at the table to share his last meal with his disciples, he said, "With desire I have desired to eat this passover with you before I suffer." (Luke 22:15, KJV) The words "desire" and "desired" in this text speak of an ardent "longing or lust" from the heart and even go so far as to speak of sexual desire. Of course, we know that Jesus was not sexually attracted to his disciples (to the pure all things are pure). However, these two words provide us with a profound revelation of Jesus' affection for those in whom he had invested his whole life. In many ways, they were "his baby," and he cared for them like a mother cares for her children and more. In the Message Bible, Jesus says, "You've no idea how much I have looked forward to eating this Passover meal with you..." and truly the disciples had no idea how much Jesus loved them like no child can begin to fathom the love his or her parents have for them. This is why his heart was set on being with his disciples; he dearly loved them and wanted to spend time with them before he went to the cross.

Have you ever wondered what kind of guest Jesus would be if he came to your home for dinner? After studying the Gospels for a number of years, I noticed that it was not at all uncommon for Jesus to be invited by someone to have dinner in their home. And as I looked close at each instance, I started to see what kind of guest he really was in each situation. Then, I asked myself: How would he behave, and what kind of things would he say if I invited him over for dinner in my house to eat with me and my family and friends?

Wherever he went, the Father went. When he entered a house, the Kingdom poured out through him in blessing, healing, deliverance, and truth. His words and actions were always unusual, depending on who surrounded Him. But when we understand everything he said and did, from Heaven's perspective, it all reveals the grace of love and restoration.

He always had a way of making things interesting.

For example, his first miracle took place at a wedding feast where he turned water into wine. Apparently, Jesus loved parties because, in those days, if the wine ran out the party stopped (John 2:1-10). Then, there were two occasions, after his resurrection, while eating with his disciples, that he cooked a fish-n-bread breakfast, asked hard questions, opened spiritual eyes, and delivered some of his most profound teachings (John 21:9-23; Luke 24:30-31). And there were other times, in people's homes, when he cast out demons, healed the blind and mute, forgave sin, restored paralytics, taught hard truths in strange ways, behaved like a madman, rebuked the religious, denied sign-seekers, and judged the wicked (See Matthew 12:22-13:1; Mark 2:1-12). He certainly had a way of making every meal supernatural (Luke 24:36-49).

> When we understand everything he said and did, from Heaven's perspective, it all reveals the grace of love and restoration.

As you read over the following short-stories ask yourself the following questions:

Would I invite Jesus over to my house for dinner? What would he be like if he came to my house and had dinner with me and my loved-ones? What would happen? What would he say? What would he do? How would I response? What if he wasn't the ideal guest who met all the standards of social propriety? What if he wasn't at all what I expected? What if he made me look bad in front of everyone?

This study will give us a foretaste of the nature of Jesus Christ in personal visitation. When he appears in the manifestation of his divine Presence, to meet with us in the place of personal and corporate visitation, he is always himself, but not like you may think.

The time will come when Jesus will get very close to you, and when it happens, he will get in "your space." Are you ready for that? Well, perhaps the following stories will help you prepare for that moment. I pray it helps you as it has helped me.

"Pete's Diner"

After "church" one day, Jesus went to Peter's house and saw his mother-in-law lying down, sick with a fever. This obviously troubled the entire household, including Peter and his wife. But what did Jesus do? How did he respond? He brought the Kingdom of God to her life - he broke the fever by touching her hand. He lifted her up and made her whole again, in more ways than one. Then, after immediately being healed, she got up and, out of gratitude, started fixing dinner for Jesus and everyone who was present. Later, after word had spread that Jesus was in town, after the sun had set, crowds of people began to descend on that house, bringing their sick and demon possessed to be healed by him (Matthew 8:14-17; Mark 1:29-34; Luke 4:38-39). They gathered at the door, waiting for the chance to be changed forever. Can you imagine this scene in your mind? Can you picture it happening in your average house, in your average little town, anywhere in the world? Can you imagine it happening in your home?

Jesus cast out all the demons with "a word" and healed everyone who was sick with various diseases. He exercised unlimited authority over the powers of darkness without breaking a sweat. Can you fathom the excitement of that evening? That house, hours earlier in the day, wasn't special in any way compared to any other house, but when Jesus came in he made all things new and changed the lives of all who filled it.

But then again, Jesus had a knack for changing everyone he ever touched, including the religious leaders. As far as we know, Jesus was invited on three separate occasions by Pharisees to eat in their homes. Each story has its own twist, showing a different side of Jesus each time.

Pharisee #1
Dinner at Simon's
(When the whore became holy)

In Luke 7:36-50, Jesus was invited by Simon, a Pharisee, to eat dinner at his home. After accepting his offer Jesus went to Simon's house, sat down at the table, and within moments was approached by the local harlot. Can you imagine how this looked to everyone present? Obviously, this woman would never have done this if Jesus wasn't there in the first place, because the religious leaders were legalists when it came to sinners. But now after seeking love in all the wrong places (both in the "church" and on the street), she was with Love Himself and all she could do was worship. After she heard that Jesus was a guest in this Pharisee's home, she mustered up all the courage she had within herself and took a leap of faith. She entered the house, walked past all the judgmental eyes, stood at his feet behind him, and with the tears that were pouring from her eyes, she washed his feet, kissed them with all the affection she had in her heart, and oiled them with costly perfume.

When Simon, the Pharisee, saw this, he thought within himself, "If this guy was truly prophetic, he'd know what kind of woman this is who is kissing and fondling his feet so inappropriately in front of everyone. Does he not realize how bad this looks?"

Apparently, Simon had no idea, at that moment, how intuitive Jesus really was; if he had, he would have known that Jesus heard every critical thought he just had. But then, he had a rude awakening when Jesus said, "Simon, I have something to say to you." I can almost hear Simon taking a deep gulp as he replied, "Oh? What is it?" I think deep down inside Simon knew his dinner guest was about to rock his legalistic boat. So Jesus told him a story that beautifully illustrated to everyone the motivation behind this sinner's actions: gratitude. For the first time ever, after being consistently rejected by the religious establishment, she finally found someone who loved her beyond her mess, beyond her faults and filthiness; for the first time she was safe with someone she could trust with all her heart, who would make her brand new from the inside out; for the first time, she found forgiveness, and this single act of worship was the only way she could possibly say, "Thank you." She had no words to express what she felt; all she could do was show it. So she subjected herself to unspeakable scorn when she walked into that dining room full of self-righteous bigots in order to get to her savior, and she sacrificed the perfume which was perhaps her most valuable commodity. But Jesus was on her side. So he put Simon in his place and turned to the woman who was still weeping and kissing his feet and said, "I forgive you," for all to hear. Of course, this upset the dinner guests who immediately started murmuring behind Jesus' back, saying, "Who does this guy think he is to forgive sin? What arrogance! Does he think

> Jesus always had a way of...blessing people in ways that felt like anything but a blessing.

he's God?" But Jesus was unmoved. He ignored them, and with all the grace of restoration behind him, said to the woman, "Your faith has saved you. Go in peace."

I'm sure Simon had no idea what he was in for when he invited Jesus over for dinner. I suppose he thought they would have a civilized, religious conversation that would appeal to everyone. I suppose he thought Jesus would bless, encourage, and grace them with his presence. The truth is he did, but not as they had hoped. Jesus always had a way of shattering religious expectations and blessing people in ways that felt like anything but a blessing. When Jesus entered that home, he brought the Kingdom with him and changed everything: he rebuked the religious and purified the prostitute; he judged the judgmental and forgave the judged.

What if Jesus came over to your house for dinner? Would you invite him over as your guest of honor?

Pharisee #2
The Legalists & the Unsavory Guest

In Luke 11:37-54, after Jesus gave one of the strongest words of judgment he ever gave, he was invited by another Pharisee to join him at his home for dinner. Why? What did he want? Was he not paying attention to his last sermon? Apparently, he thought Jesus wouldn't "be himself" in his home. Well, he was sadly mistaken (as the religious crew always was and still is).

When Jesus accepted the invitation, he went to the house and sat down at the table without washing his hands, which was a no-no according to Jewish custom. Needless to say, this shocked his host and all the other guests. Certainly, Jesus knew that when you are invited to someone's home for dinner, you ought to respect "the rules of the house." How could Jesus be so rude and uncivilized? Where were his manners? Why would he do such a thing? Didn't his mom raise him better than that? Obviously, he owed his host an explanation.

And that is exactly what he did when he said, "Now you Pharisees cleanse the outside of the cup and of the plate, but inside you yourselves are full of greed and robbery and extortion and malice and wickedness. You senseless (foolish, stupid) ones [acting without reflection or intelligence]! Did not He Who made the outside make the inside also? But [dedicate your inner self and] give as donations to the poor of those things which are within [of inward righteousness] and behold, everything is purified and clean for you. But woe to you, Pharisees! For you tithe mint and rue and every [little] herb, but disregard and neglect justice and the love of God. These you ought to have done without leaving the others undone. Woe to you, Pharisees! For you love the best seats in the synagogues and [you love] to be greeted and bowed down to in the [public] marketplaces. Woe to you! For you are like graves which are not marked or seen, and men walk over them without being aware of it [and are ceremonially defiled]" (Luke 11:39-44, Amp)

Well, Jesus really knew how to sweet-talk someone didn't he? He was invited by this religious leader into their home for dinner, and Jesus verbally slapped him and his religious buddies in front of God and everyone. Can you imagine if something like this were to happen in the house of your average religious leader today? What do you think the response would be? If you were there, would you stand with or against Jesus? Would you think he was being too heavy-handed, too harsh, too mean? Where was "sweet and gentle Jesus"? Obviously, Jesus was right in what he said and how he said it, but at the time it sure didn't "feel" right to everyone. We know this because one of the religious lawyers then piped in and voiced his outrage; they knew what Jesus was saying to the Pharisee applied to all the religious leaders, and they did not like it. They didn't appreciate being insulted and exposed. But Jesus didn't hold back:

"Woe to you, the lawyers, also! For you load men with oppressive burdens hard to bear, and you do not personally [even gently] touch the burdens with one of your fingers. Woe to you! For you are rebuilding and repairing the tombs of the prophets, whom your fathers killed (destroyed). So you bear witness and give your full approval and consent to the deeds of your fathers; for they actually killed them, and you rebuild and repair monuments to them. For this reason also the wisdom of God said, I will send them prophets and apostles, [some] of whom they will put to death and persecute, so that the blood of all the prophets shed from the foundation of the world may be charged against and required of this age and generation, from the blood of Abel to the blood of Zechariah, who was slain between the altar and the sanctuary. Yes, I tell you, it shall be charged against and required of this age and generation. Woe to you, lawyers (experts in the Mosaic Law)! For you have taken away the key to knowledge; you did not go in yourselves, and you hindered and prevented those who were entering" (Luke 11:46-52, Amp).

Jesus knew the oppressive nature of the religious leaders – he had observed the byproducts of their religious system over the course of thirty-years of living side-by-side with it – and now he was calling them out, divulging their wickedness. But of all the places he could have chosen to have this show-down, why did he choose dinner-time in the house of a Pharisee? Why did he use a time that was and is usually meant for food and light-hearted fellowship? Why would Jesus insult the host and his religious associates while in his home? Did he not know how it was going to end? Did he think they were going to repent after being brow-beaten and publically mortified? Did he not know that they were going to be enraged by his words so much that they began to plot against him? Well, they did, and it eventually took his life.

So, again, what if Jesus came over to your house for dinner? Would you invite him over a second time?

Pharisee #3
The Test

On a third and final occasion, Jesus shared a meal in the house of another Pharisee, who was actually one of the top leaders of the Pharisee sect (See Luke 14:1-24). But this particular get-together was a trap from the beginning, covered up by the debris of a seemingly innocent dinner invitation!

From the moment Jesus entered the house, the host and all his religious guests had their eyes on him, closely watching his every move. They didn't really want to spend time with him because they liked him or because he had something they wanted. They had heard his words, seen his actions, and knew where he stood, and now they were up to no good. So they lured him in and ambushed him with human bait. They put a man who was massively swollen in his joints right in front of Jesus to see what he was going to do. Of course, they didn't make it obvious that this was a test, but Jesus knew it and purposefully failed it, for everyone's benefit. They wanted to see if Jesus would actually

> What if Jesus came over to your house for dinner? Would you invite him over a second time?

break their Sabbath law by healing this man, and that is exactly what he did but not before he asked his host and fellow guests, "Is it lawful and right to cure on the Sabbath or not?" (Amp) Of course, the religious leaders had nothing to say. They were stumped. So Jesus, instead of debating with them, showed them the "right" thing to do. He touched the sick man, healed him, and sent him on his way. Then to seal the deal, he asked his audience, "Which of you, having a son or a donkey or an ox that has fallen into a well, will not at once pull him out on the Sabbath day?" (Amp) Again, no one could answer him, but their silence spoke louder than words ever could. They loved the law more than the hurting but loved their children, donkeys, and oxen enough to break their esteemed law. Somehow this man with dropsy wasn't worth their love. So Jesus purposefully exposed their hypocrisy.

He then shifted his attention to the guests who, as he had noticed, all tried to sit in the highest places of honor at the dinner table. He could tell they were high on themselves by the way they elbowed their way to the best seats in the house; to them, this banquet wasn't about fellowship but rather social-climbing. So, true to form, he proceeded to expose and rebuke them too, en mass, saying, "When you are invited by anyone to a marriage feast, do not recline on the chief seat [in the place of honor], lest a more distinguished person than you has been invited by him, and he who invited both of you will come to you and say, Let this man have the place [you have taken]. Then, with humiliation and a guilty sense of impropriety, you will begin to take the lowest place. But when you are invited, go and recline in the lowest place, so that when your host comes in, he may say to you, Friend, go up higher! Then you will be honored in the presence of all who sit [at table] with you. For everyone who exalts himself will be humbled (ranked below others who are honored or rewarded), and he who humbles himself (keeps a modest opinion of himself and behaves accordingly) will be exalted (elevated in rank)." (Amp) Jesus knew their hearts, but they didn't know who he was; if they had, they would have offered him the best seat in the house, way before themselves. Their actions revealed their true nature to Jesus. He saw their pride and went for the jugular.

Then, he turned to his host and embarrassed him in front of everyone by telling him who he should and should not have invited for dinner. He said, "When you give a dinner or a supper, do not invite your friends or your brothers or your relatives or your wealthy neighbors, lest perhaps they also invite you in return, and so you are paid back. But when you give a banquet or a reception, invite the poor, the disabled, the lame, and the blind. Then you will be blessed (happy, fortunate, and to be envied), because they have no way of repaying you, and you will be recompensed at the resurrection of the just (upright)." (Amp) In other words, Jesus said, "You invited your well-to-do friends and family and neglected the needy, for selfish gain. You give because you want not because you care; if you really cared, you would give to those who can't return the favor. From now on, if you want to be blessed, pour yourself out for those who cannot bless you. Then my father will reward you."

After hearing this, one of the guests said to Jesus, "Blessed (happy, fortunate, and to be envied) is he who shall eat bread in the kingdom of God!" (Amp) Obviously, this person agreed with what Jesus was saying and was affirming his words, but I also sense that they were subtly attempting to broaden the way to the Kingdom of God which Jesus was always narrowing. How do I know this? Because Jesus responded to the man by saying, "A man was once giving a great supper and invited many; and at the hour for the supper he sent his servant to say to those who had been invited, Come, for all is now ready. But they all alike began to make excuses and to beg off. The first said to him, I have bought a piece of land, and I have to go out and see it; I beg you, have me excused. And another said, I have bought five yoke of oxen, and I am going to examine and put my approval on them; I beg you, have me excused. And another said, I have married a wife, and because of this I am unable to come. So the servant came and reported these [answers] to his master. Then the master of the house said in wrath to his servant, Go quickly into the great streets and the small streets of the city and bring in here the poor and the disabled and the blind and the lame. And the servant [returning] said, Sir, what you have commanded me to do has been done, and yet there is room. Then the master said to the servant, Go out into the highways and hedges and urge and constrain [them] to yield and come in, so that my house may be filled. For I tell you, not one of those who were invited shall taste my supper" (Amp).

So, when the guest mentioned how blessed are those who eat bread in the Kingdom of God, Jesus basically said, "Yes, but the only ones who will eat in my house when they are invited are those who are desperate for help in their lives because they cannot help themselves. The self-sufficient and affluent in this world will not be blessed in my World but those who truly need me in this world will be blessed. I want everyone to be saved. I want my house to be filled to the brim. That is why I am inviting everyone to come to my table, but few are willing to pay the price. Only those who are detached from this world and the things and people of this world will come. Only the poor in spirit will inherit the Kingdom." Jesus' answer was an attempt to raise the bar by adjusting the religious mindset of his audience which fostered a greasy, all-inclusive entrance into the Kingdom of God. He set the record straight, separating the sheep from the goats (See Matthew 25:32-46).

So in summary, Jesus, the guest of honor in the home of one of the Pharisees' top-dogs, single-handedly broke the Sabbath, rebuked the host, insulted his fellow guests, and exalted the reprobates of society – all in one evening. As Philip Yancey wrote in his book, *The Jesus I Never Knew*, "Jesus hardly made for a soothing dinner guest."

He narrowed and straightened the way to the Kingdom of God, drawing a fine line in the sand between the legalists and the lovers, the thoughtless and the thoughtful, the selfish and the selfless, the some-bodies and the no-bodies, the needless and the needful. He looked at those who say they are "rich, and increased with goods, and have need of nothing" and saw their true condition as being "wretched, and miserable, and poor, and blind, and naked" (Revelation 3:17, KJV). And he looked at those who are "the poor of this world," who are "poor in spirit," and deemed them "rich in faith and heirs of the kingdom which He promised to those who love Him?" (James 2:5; Matthew 5:3, NKJV).

So, let me ask the question again: What if Jesus came over to your house for dinner? Would you invite him over at all, knowing what you now know?

Dinner at Zach's

On one occasion, when Jesus passed through Jericho, he was being followed by a crowd that wanted to see this man they had heard so much about. But there was a rich tax collector in the crowd who was "vertically challenged" (in other words, he was short), who couldn't see Jesus but desperately wanted to. He sensed something in Jesus that was beyond him and his wealth. I believe he knew there was a hole in his heart and needed something or someone to fill it, and there was something about Jesus that drew him in like a magnet. So, following his heart, he climbed a sycamore tree that Jesus was about to pass by which lined him up for a God-encounter. As Jesus approached, he noticed this curious mini-man in the tree and said, "Zacchaeus, hurry and come down; for I must stay at your house today."

Can you imagine Jesus calling you by name and then insisting he stay at your house? Can you fathom the feelings that would rush through your heart? No wonder "Zach" rushed down that tree so fast and welcomed Jesus into his home so joyfully.

Of course, the crowd didn't like this at all. They began muttering and complaining about Jesus' choice of friends, wondering why he was lodging with a person who, in their eyes, was devoted to sin; they saw him as a thug, murderer, and reprobate.

But Zach didn't pay them any mind. He was focused on hosting this man who somehow knew him; he had spent so much of his time running after riches, but now he was with someone who had something he didn't, something money could never buy. Being in the presence of Jesus did something to him; it began to change him, from the inside out, until he was so stirred that he stood up in the middle of their time together in his home and said, "See, Lord, the half of my goods I [now] give [by way of restoration] to the poor, and if I have cheated anyone out of anything, I [now] restore four times as much." Can you picture in your mind what this looked like? What a scene! Zach and Jesus were spending time together in a room along with "the poor" and those Zach had apparently "cheated" in the past, and suddenly he gets up and starts giving to the poor and righting wrongs. What a transformation!

After being with Jesus for a short time, Zach was a changed man. He was truly "born again," and it was so genuine that Jesus declared "Today is…salvation come to [all the members of] this household, since Zacchaeus too is a [real spiritual] son of Abraham; for the Son of Man came to seek and to save that which was lost."

Zach was a new man, and his whole family was saved as a result of his radical reformation; he went from being a son of greed to a real son of Abraham (I wonder what the Jews, who believed *they* were the real children of Abraham, thought about this.). He was delivered from his old life. Old things passed away and all things became new at that very moment. He didn't care anymore about "stuff" and "money" but rather became driven by righteousness and goodness through spending a few minutes with the greatest Change Agent of all time.

Like the religious leaders of his day, Zach was curious about this man, Jesus, but he was far more than curious; he was desperate to have the void in his life filled with something more, far beyond what he already had or thought he had. His heart was open to the Lord – teachable, vulnerable, and honest – and the Lord rewarded him with a brand new life.

Jesus always graced the humble and resisted the proud. He invested the best of himself in those whose hearts were as good, rich ground and never cast his pearls to pigs. Zach's humility positioned him for grace from God. He laid down his greatness, because he finally found someone who was greater than anything or anyone he had ever known. He was desperate for "more," for a change, for a new life because he was tired of the endless cycle of death he was in.

Are you desperate yet? Are you ready for a complete make-over?

If not, let us take a look at another man who was changed from the inside out.

Dinner at Levi's

After healing a man who was paralyzed, Jesus moved on from that place and noticed a man named Matthew (a.k.a. Levi) who was sitting in a tax office. Luke's gospel, in the Amp Bible, says Jesus "looked attentively" at this man who was a tax collector by trade. Like the paralyzed man Jesus had just healed, Levi was paralyzed as well, in his heart, but all of that was about to change.

What did Jesus see in Levi? He didn't look at everyone like that, but there was something about Levi that grabbed his attention in such a way that he went over to Levi and said, "Follow me!" Notice, he didn't ask Levi if he wanted to follow him – he told him. But Levi didn't seem to care that he was being ordered around by this complete stranger because, somehow, deep inside, he knew this man; something in him clicked when their eyes met. In fact, it seems Levi was so taken with Jesus (as Jesus was likewise taken with Levi), that he got up from where he was, left everything, and followed him without being together beforehand where they were going. Clearly, Jesus had something Levi wanted more than everything he already had; or there was something about Jesus that just made sense more than anything he had ever known.

> Zach's heart was open to the Lord – teachable, vulnerable and honest – and the Lord rewarded him with a brand new life.

So Levi hosted a large dinner at his home for Jesus. And, as always, Jesus attracted a mixed crowd of tax collectors and "especially wicked sinners" who sat down with him and his disciples at the dinner table (Matthew 9:10, Amp). For the first time, this unsavory group of misfits had someone who really loved them and actually liked them enough to hang out with them on their level, despite their mess. This, of course, as always, offended the religious crowd who complained to Jesus' disciples that they should not have been eating and drinking with such riff-raff. When Jesus heard their murmuring, he said to them "Those who are strong and well (healthy) have no need of a physician, but those who are weak and sick. Go and learn what this means: I desire mercy [that is, readiness to help those in trouble] and not sacrifice and sacrificial victims. For I came not to call and invite [to repentance] the righteous (those who are upright and in right standing with God), but sinners (the erring ones and all those not free from sin)." (Amp)

Notice, Jesus didn't sweep their sin under the carpet, but neither was he passing judgment from a distance; he loved them enough to unconditionally love them into freedom through companionship. He surrounded himself with those who were enslaved to impurity and "the almighty dollar" because he knew he had something within him that could free them from all their bondage, if they wanted it. He saw who these people really were beyond what everyone else saw and set them up, through relationship with him, to be recipients of his higher life.

Unlike the religious leaders who were in the room, Jesus didn't require these derelicts to jump through any religious hoops before they were qualified to be in his presence. They just wanted to be with him, and he let them into his circle knowing that his presence was all they really needed to bring them into their potential in him.

But since Jesus' answer to the Pharisees first question was so good, shaming them in front of everyone by putting their true motives on display, someone cut in and asked a question that was completely off the subject; needless to say, they were bound and determined to catch Jesus off-guard:

"The disciples of John practice fasting often and offer up prayers...and so do [the disciples] of the Pharisees...but yours eat and drink." (Amp) In other words, "All the other 'true believers' are fasting and praying so much more than you guys are. Are you guys serious about your faith?"

Jesus answered, "Can you make the wedding guests fast as long as the bridegroom is with them? But the days will come when the bridegroom will be taken from them; and then they will fast in those days" (Amp). Jesus then used two obscure parables (The new patch with the old garment and the new wine with the old wineskin) to further rebuke the religious community for mismatching spiritual disciplines with spiritual seasons; if they had noticed the "Bridegrooms" presence, they would not have been praying and fasting as if he was absent; as always, they failed to discern the signs of the times and were thus irrelevant in their day (Matthew 16:3).

Jesus didn't pull any punches, but his attention was primarily on the sinners who were in the room. Think about it: who invited Jesus and his disciples for dinner? Levi! Who else was at the party? Crooks, sinners, and religious leaders. Who ruined the dinner-party? The religious leaders. They nit-picked everything they could find, and Jesus put them in their place in short-order, right in front of everyone, because he was set on loving over legalizing hurting lives. [This story can be found in Matthew 9:9-19; Mark 2:14-22; Luke 5:27-39]

Martha & Mary

During one of Jesus' visits to Bethany, he and his disciples were invited by Martha to have dinner in her home. Unlike most who misunderstood and rejected Jesus without even really knowing who he was, Martha saw how special he was, embraced him, and opened her home to him. She and her younger sister, Mary, both loved Jesus very much but in very different ways.

Mary spent the whole night sitting at Jesus' feet, listening to every word he said. She wasn't interested in fixing dinner or eating food. But she was hungry; her heart wanted something else, something more. She wanted to be with Jesus. Her affection for Jesus was extraordinary and she couldn't hide it (See John 12:1-9).

Martha, on the other hand, was busy in the kitchen anxiously preparing a large meal for Jesus, his disciples, Mary, herself, and possibly Lazarus; she was so focused on dinner that she was distracted from her guest of honor. Then, when she noticed that Mary wasn't helping her, she got upset, walked over to Jesus, and said, "Lord, is it nothing to you that my sister has left me to serve alone? Tell her then to help me [to lend a hand and do her part along with me]!" (Amp) Notice how she blamed Jesus for not caring about her plight as the lone hostess? She accused him of being unfair and then demanded that Jesus tell her sister to pitch-in. Martha was so focused on what she was doing that she thought the whole evening revolved around her.

Now understand, in those days homes where divided into male space and female space. The kitchen belonged to the women. The main room was for the men, and it was considered improper, even scandalous, for a woman to be in there except for a short period of time. The only place where men and women could be together was the master bedroom. So, when Mary was seated at Jesus' feet with the disciples in the public room, she "crossed the line" because she sat where only men belonged. Moreover, she sat at his feet as a disciple, which was also taboo since every rabbi in that day only had male disciples (Of course, this means Jesus also broke "the rule" since he discipled men and women throughout his ministry).

Mary was so desperate for "more" of Jesus that she broke tradition. Of course, Martha did not understand this; she was "in her place," slaving in the kitchen while her sister was, essentially, acting like a man! Martha understood proper etiquette and was so disgusted with her little sister's impropriety that she demanded Jesus to make it right.

So what did Jesus do? Did he use his authority to demand Mary's service and affirm Martha's complaint? Did he say, "You know, Martha, you're right! You've been working so hard and Mary's been rude and too 'spiritual' to help you. Where are

> Mary was so desperate for "more" of Jesus that she broke tradition.

my manners? Martha, please forgive me for being so inconsiderate. Mary, help your sister." No! Instead, he said, "Oh Martha, Martha, you're bothered about so many things but there's only one thing that really matters. Mary understands this and has made up her mind. She has chosen the 'main course' of the meal I have prepared for all of you – ME! – and it won't be taken from her." It seems that Jesus didn't even notice Martha's good intentions. Instead, he looked into her heart, saw who she really was, saw her core motivations, and brought everything to the surface. Her service was misguided because her heart was misdirected. [This story can be found in Luke 10:38-42]

Martha welcomed Jesus into her home – her world – as "the woman of the house," and went to work trying to serve him to the best of her ability. But, when the time came to be a disciple – to sit, be still, and listen to him – when the time came to enjoy him, to be "at home" with him, she missed it. She failed to discern the purpose of that moment. Mary was concerned about "one thing" – being with Jesus and knowing him (See Psalm 27:4, 8). Jesus accepted Martha's invitation because he wanted to be with them. He was more interested, at that moment, in intimate fellowship than in eating good food and talking about the weather. So, when Martha became distracted from the real reason they were together, Jesus basically said, "Martha, stop what you're doing, relax, and be with me. I came to be with you."

Closer to Home

Does *this* Jesus resemble the Jesus you heard about in Sunday School growing up? When was the last time anyone showed you this side of him? Or have you never heard of *this* Jesus?

Of course, please understand, it's not that the Jesus we heard about was all wrong, only incomplete, thanks to the influences of our self-centered, religious, western culture. Therefore, when the topic of Christlikeness comes up, we paint an incomplete picture for "believers" of what it means to be like him. But what if we considered the other parts of his life that have been conveniently overlooked by all of us and revisited what it means to be like him, to be a true Christian? I know it can be disconcerting, to say the least, to see Jesus beyond the pigeon-holed version we've been fed, but if, as John said, we will become like him when we see him as he is, then will we not be transformed into his likeness and image to the degree that we see him? I don't know about you, but I refuse to let anything keep me from seeing him more and more clearly so that I can fulfill my potential on this side of heaven.

Did you notice, after reading the stories above, the stark contrast between Jesus' behavior toward the everyday-person and the religious busy-body? It was like night and day! He rarely had any compassion on the self-righteous folk, especially the religious clergy of his day, while he loved on the broken. He condemned the proud and spent himself on the humble. The only ones Jesus seemed to be in sync with were those who were desperate and teachable, who needed help and deliverance. And since most people were conceited and hard-hearted (and still are), he incidentally ended up slighting most of his hosts.

So, the question that's begging to be asked is, what if Jesus came to your house? Would you like him at first and then hate him later after he loved you enough to tell you the truth, exposing your closeted skeletons in the process? Would you be meek enough to let him speak into your life even when it pains your pride or religious mind? How would you respond to Jesus' pitiable protocol? What if you made him dinner, and he repaid you with a rebuke? Would you be offended? What if he didn't let you hide or run from the Truth in your house, your domain? Would you ever have him over again?

Well, let's bring this closer to home...

What if a real Christian – a truly Christ-like individual (Romans 8:19) – came into your house? What if they entered your personal space and, like Jesus, only spoke what they heard our Father saying and only did what they saw our Father doing? What if they treated you the way you needed to be treated instead of the way wanted to be treated? How would their words and actions affect you? Would you get defensive? Would your feelings get hurt and get in the way of receiving them for who they are to you in Christ? Would their presence in your life not be for a reason? Do you believe in divine appointments?

Those who are truly following Jesus will not be like everyone else; in fact, they will be judged in the same way Jesus was judged, as a crazy, hateful, deceived, demon-possessed individual. Few will be able to relate to them in the same way that few were able to relate to Jesus, who was like an alien from another planet. Most will stiff-arm them, except those who are broken and contrite enough to discern their hearts and the fruit of their lives.

When someone starts behaving in ways that resemble Jesus' life, as we have seen, be careful not to write them off too quickly. They may not be what you want them to be, but that doesn't mean they aren't what our Father wants them to be. Just because someone makes you unhappy doesn't mean they are displeasing to the Lord. This is why we must become more sensitive to God's heart than we are to our own and everyone else's.

I pray that we will not be afraid to become more like him, and that we will not reject others who are more like him than we are simply because we don't like their method or manner. In the end, humility will be the primary virtue that will give us the grace to keep us from running away from him, no matter who he comes through. And as he makes us more like him, his love for us will be the only thing that will keep us strong when it seems we're all alone for simply being who he made us to be.

- 5 -

Jesus Goes To Church

S he was sitting on the floor in her room, spending time with the Lord, crying. Of course, I didn't understand why – I was four years old. So I asked her if she was sad. She said she was crying because she loved Jesus which raised my curiosity even more. I saw something in her that I wanted. I had to know him. So mom introduced me to her friend, the one who knew her best and loved her most. That was the beginning of a journey that has conditioned my whole life with him to such a degree that I've remained, for the most part, unsatisfied with anything less than the pure love he gave me the day we met.

And yet, throughout my life, there have been times when "religion" has tried to creep into my mind and heart to make me somehow think I needed something else. And there were times when I bought the lie and, without knowing it, headed away from the Lord down a path that was fun, on the surface, laden with "good" things, such as church activities, programs, events, etc. Then, in addition to all that, I read all the right books, attended all the cutting-edge, deeper-life conventions and conferences, listened to all the teaching tapes I could get my hands on, and went to church faithfully, every time the doors were open, like a good Christian. But still, something was wrong. Something was missing.

Over and over again, well-meaning church people warned me not to forsake the assembling of myself with the people of God, as if going to church was the only way to assemble. And yet, as much as I went to church to try and submit to their counsel, thinking they were right, I found myself surrounded by people I didn't know at all. Fellowshipping with the back of someone's head in the pews, sharing short and shallow conversations on the way to

"Sunday School" or "The Sanctuary," passing the offering plate back and forth, going through the same boringly uniform motions every Sunday and finally running out the door after "The Service" to get to the local restaurant before the church crowds converged, felt more like a social club than the vibrant, personal interaction of a family that's deeply in-love. Somehow, inside, I knew we had lowered the bar on "fellowship."

Then, one day, I was drawn to the Gospels and started reading them over and over again, and I couldn't stop. I felt like a junkie looking for his next fix. I couldn't get enough, and I knew Jesus' life had the answers to all my questions, even the questions I wasn't asking but soon would. For a long time I couldn't read anything except the Gospels which put me in a place, spiritually and mentally, where his life started to confront and transform my thinking in many ways regarding church-life (and life in general). And as I gradually began to see his life and the life he shared with his followers who were really his friends, without all the religious noise and bombast, the purity, clarity, and simplicity of Christ's definition of fellowship, "church" and church-life began to shine through. The more I read, the freer I became, and since I was fed up with religion's sop, I knew Jesus' life alone had the key. For a long time I didn't feel it was time to share what I discovered and am still discovering, but now is the time.

> Jesus' life has the answers to all our questions, even the questions we aren't asking but soon will.

What you are about to read is a peek into some of what I found.

Sunday Mornin' Homecomin'

After being baptized in the Jordan and spending forty days and forty nights in the desert, Jesus returned in the power of the Spirit to Galilee and started teaching in their "churches." And apparently he was such an excellent teacher that he quickly became front-page news.

Then he went home, to Nazareth, probably thinking his hometown would like the "new me" as much as the people of Galilee. So he went to "church" on "Sunday" to make his grand debut, but it didn't take long before things turned ugly.

Remember, Nazareth was his home town, the place where he cut his teeth, went to school, played with friends, and eventually became a man. Everyone knew who he was. They saw him when he was in diapers, spitting up baby food and making a mess. They had gone to "church" with him every "Sunday" since he was born.

> Jesus went to "church" on "Sunday" to make his grand debut, but it didn't take long before things turned ugly.

But this "Sunday" was different.

When Jesus entered "The Sanctuary," he approached the "pulpit," opened his "Bible" to Isaiah 61:1-2, and started reading out loud:

"The Spirit of the Lord [is] upon Me, because He has anointed Me [the Anointed one, the Messiah] to preach the good news (the Gospel) to the poor; He has sent Me to announce release to the captives and recovery of sight to the blind, to send forth as delivered those who are oppressed [who are downtrodden, bruised, crushed, and broken down by calamity], to proclaim the accepted and acceptable year of the Lord [the day when salvation and the free favors of God profusely abound.]" (Amp).

Then, apparently, at some point during "the meeting," Jesus displayed miraculous powers that were so amazing that everyone wondered where he got them. And his words were so full of grace and wisdom that everyone marveled. Obviously, this wasn't the same Jesus they were used to. Yet, when he finished reading Isaiah's prophecy, he closed the book, sat down, and with all eyes watching, said, "Today this Scripture is fulfilled in your hearing." In other words, he said, "This passage is talking about me. You don't have to wait for it to be fulfilled anymore. I am the Messiah."

Of course, everyone was stunned. How could Jesus be the Messiah? To them, he was simply "the carpenter." They knew his mom and dad and brothers and sisters by name. How could he possibly be the fulfillment of Isaiah's prophecy?

Then, to make matters worse, Jesus spoke of himself as a prophet without honor in his own hometown and topped it off by essentially comparing himself to some of Israel's greatest prophets, Elijah and Elisha, which so infuriated everyone that they kicked him out of town and tried to throw him over a cliff. These "believers," who had been his neighbors his whole life, became so enraged by what he said that they wanted him dead as soon as possible. And yet, when they attempted to kill him, he gave them the slip and finally went back to Galilee and ministered in their churches where the reception was, well, less hostile (See Luke 4:16-37 as well as Matthew 13:54-58; Mark 6:1-6).

The "church" in Nazareth had their own ideas of how Isaiah 61:1-2 was going to pan out and Jesus didn't come close to matching it. They put their own spin on what God had in mind and as a result missed entirely the blessings that were included in the prophecy.

Nazareth was so familiar with his humanity, so preoccupied with how "different" he was and so satisfied with "business as usual," that they failed to notice that he had come "in the name of the Lord," the One they professed to follow (Matthew 23:39, KJV).

He possessed all the answers to all their problems. He offered healing, deliverance, restoration, and blessing. But all they cared about was that he was unsettling their comfortable religious world. They believed he was narcissistic and delusional and were so offended by him that they were hindered from being able to recognize his authority.

As a result, he was accepted in Galilee where he could be himself and was despised in Nazareth where he "could do no mighty work…except that He laid His hands on a few sick people and healed them." (Mark 6:5, NKJV)

Today, there are many churches like the "church" in Nazareth which only saw what it was prepared to see and missed the time of their visitation because God came to them in a form they never expected (Luke 19:44). Then, on the flip side, there are churches like the "church" in Galilee, where Jesus can be himself, no matter how he comes, no matter what he looks like, no matter how contrary he is to what they're used to or what they've been told. The main difference between the two is that one discerns him after the flesh, while the other discerns him after the Spirit; one judges him by what's been done before, while the other judges him by his fruit.

Mr. Alien

The story you just read was one of many similar occurrences. Every time Jesus and "religion" or "church" connected, they mixed like oil and water. Why? Because church-folk didn't like him, and there was nothing in him or about him that affirmed their culture or paradigm. Though he preached in many "churches" throughout the course of his ministry-life, he never "fit in." He was a square peg surrounded by round holes, always going against the grain. And what's funny is that he irritated religious people by just being himself. Even at the age of twelve, he had a special way of dropping pious jaws (Luke 2:46-47). If only he had been anyone but himself, he wouldn't have caused so much trouble.

Unlike most ministers today, Jesus wasn't "seeker sensitive." He didn't meet people where they were by giving them what they "wanted" or "preferred" so they would like him or so that he wouldn't offend them. And he was never concerned about growing and maintaining a "following." Rather, he was sensitive to the guidance of his Father who always sought to meet people at their deepest point of "need" – way below the surface.

> While everyone around Jesus revered the religious establishment and all its trappings, he did not, which so freed him from all that blinds, that he was able to see through things much more quickly and clearly than everyone around Him.

While everyone around Jesus revered the religious establishment and all its trappings, he did not, which so freed him from all that blinds, that he was able to see through things much more quickly and clearly than everyone around Him. He could walk into any "church" and immediately discern the primary root or roots to any and every problem; and most of the time he would expose everything hidden in darkness, even to his own hurt and eventual death.

When Jesus "went to church," he brought the living reality of his World with him by living on earth as he lived in Heaven, behaving according to his identity in his Father. In other words, he was like an alien in a foreign world or like a rose in a garden of weeds, even though the weeds thought they were the roses and he was the weed.

His presence made everyone uncomfortable, except for the humble, because he was unconventional in every way, igniting fierce resistance everywhere he went. He never went with the flow in order to avoid the path of least resistance. He didn't "go along to get along." While religious leaders expected everything in "church" to be "decent and in order," Jesus behaved in ways that seemed grossly inappropriate and messy. By religious standards, he always did what "ought not be done."

For instance...

- He defied the Law of Moses, which dictated the "churches'" "bylaws," by disregarding the Sabbath (Matthew 12:1-14; Mark 2:23-28; 3:1-6; Luke 4:31-37; 6:1-11; John 5:1-18; 7:21-24; 9:14).

  He seemed to have no special regard for one day or time over another. In fact, he seemed to be even more inconsiderate of protocol on especially "holy" days (John 2:13-22; 7; 10). And on such occasions, he would often stand before large crowds and say things that dubbed him a blasphemous, demonized lunatic (John 7:20, 28-30, 37-39; 10:24-39).

  In Luke 13:10-17 Jesus delivered a woman, in "church," who had a spirit of infirmity. And there was only one person who did not like it: "The ruler of the synagogue" or, as we would call him today, the "pastor." In fact, he was so upset that he told the people, "Look, you can be healed any other day of the week, just not today, not on the Sabbath." Clearly, this "preacher" cared more about obeying the law than seeking God's best for his people. So Jesus proceeded to publically shame him and his associates by saying, "You hypocrites! You untie your ox or donkey from the stall and lead them to water on the Sabbath, but you won't even lift your little finger to help this dear woman who's been afflicted by Satan for eighteen years. What are you thinking?" Evidently, Jesus didn't have any intention on compromising or negotiating with this "pastor." He didn't say, "Okay, well, pastor, this is your church, and since you are the leader, we will respect your wishes" and he certainly didn't tell the people who needed healing, "If you need healing of any kind, come and see me any other day but today. We need to respect the pastor's wishes, and recognize his authority as a 'man of God.' He is God's anointed, and we need to honor him." No! Jesus put the principle of love before policy and protocol, which humiliated the "big dogs" and delighted the little people (Luke 13:17).

* He and his disciples ate without washing their hands, which was also against the tradition of the elders (Matthew 15:1-20; Mark 7:1-5; Luke 11:37-41).

  By and large, Jesus questioned and ignored "church" practices, laws and "bylaws" when they either got in the way of His Father's will for any given situation or became more important than the reality they may have been meant to represent. His general grievance against "religion" was that it always tried to limit and bind him and those who needed what he had.

* Jesus condemned ecclesiastical hierarchies and hypocrisies, "forms" of godliness, the use of "titles" and corresponding "entitlements," abuses of power and the exaltation of professional ministers which elevate certain "special" people above others, thereby producing a leadership/laity split among the people (See Matthew 6:1-7; 23:1-12; Mark 10:35-43; 12:38-40; Luke 11:39-44; 20:46-47; 22:24-27). Jesus' "on-earth-as-it-is-in-Heaven" mindset, which clashes with every earthly structure and organizational model, praised and modeled least-ness over greatness, humility over pride and service over being served.

  And as a direct solution to the problem, he introduced the priesthood of all believers to the world by equipping and releasing his "nameless" and "faceless" disciples into the world with the power and authority to heal the sick, cast out demons, raise the dead and preach the Good News to the poor.

- Jesus had "church" everywhere: in the fields, in homes, on mountainsides, at the temple, in synagogues, on the road, on seashores, in boats, etc. He didn't just have "church" at "church" and his "church family" reached far beyond all "church" walls (Luke 8:19-21). His whole life was one big "church service" because he didn't have a spiritual life and a secular life; his whole life was lived in relationship with his Father which influenced every moment of his life; he said and did everything out of who he really was, which never changed, depending on where he was or who he was with.

  By the way, while it is true that Jesus did periodically "go to church," there is no evidence that Jesus "went to church" every time the doors were open or even went every "Sunday" (See Luke 4:44). And yet, whenever he went to "church," he crossed the religious leadership and overturned their "sacred cows," which often made him a prime target for stone-throwers (Luke 11:37-12:1; John 8:31-59).

- He delivered offensive, blasphemous, divisive, seemingly demonic messages (e.g. Matthew 23; John 5; 7:14-24; 8:12-58; 10:22-44).

  For example, most of Jesus' "Eat my flesh" and "Drink my blood" sermon, in John 6, was preached in the synagogue in Capernaum and produced a "church split," on the spot, driving away thousands of people and leaving him alone, again, with his original twelve disciples. Why? Because his invitation to eat his flesh and drink his blood defied the Law of Moses which forbid cannibalism and the drinking of blood (Genesis 9:4-6; Leviticus 3:17; 7:26-27). According to Israel's history, eating human flesh was a result of disobedience against God, and here was Jesus, telling everyone to eat his flesh (Leviticus 26:14, 15, 29; Deuteronomy 28:53-57; 2 Kings 6:28-29; Jeremiah 19:9; Lamentations 2:20; 4:10; Ezekiel 5:10).

As usual, Jesus' words divided cities, people groups and "churches" by separating those who believed in him from those who did not (John 7:37-53; 9:39 in the Amp).

- He forgave especially wicked sinners, something everyone believed only God could do (Matthew 9:2-3; Luke 5:18-21). And now he has given us the power, in him, to remit sin (John 20:23).

- The record doesn't give us stories of Jesus tithing. It does show how he gave his life every day in service to the poor, the hurting, and the broken. He was a whole burnt offering, a living sacrifice, 24/7.

But this doesn't mean he was against monetary tithing. As you may recall, Jesus never rebuked the religious leaders for tithing. Rather, he called them "pretenders (hypocrites)!" because they gave a tenth of their resources but "neglected and omitted the weightier (more important) matters of the Law--right and justice and mercy and fidelity." (Matthew 23:23, Amp) He condemned these religious people for putting duty for God before "the love of God" which, by his very words, proves that it is possible to fulfill every pious obligation without actually loving him (Luke 11:42, Amp). Jesus never made tithing a litmus test for Christian devotion.

As for Jesus, again, he upheld a higher standard by giving 100% of himself every moment of every day. Indeed, if he had only given a tithe of himself, of his life, where would you and I be today? He gave it all and praised this quality of sacrifice in others. For example, during one of his visits to the temple, he sat down near the offering box and started watching "how" people were giving. After seeing the rich throw in large sums of money, he noticed a poverty-stricken widow who "came and put in two copper mites [the smallest of coins], which together make half of a cent." This so moved him that he called his disciples to him and praised this woman and, in effect, made an example of her. Why? Because she gave all she had to live on, she gave out of her lack, which was much more than anyone else had given, including the rich people who gave out of their wealth to appease their consciences without any real impact on their lives (Mark 12:41-44; Luke 21:1-4, Amp). Jesus' whole life was a personal gift that he and his Father gave to mankind.

- He overturned tables and drove out merchants in the Temple with a whip in hand (Matthew 21:12-13; Mark 11:15-18; Luke 19:45-46; John 2:13-17). He was a zealot for the Kingdom of God, but he didn't carry daggers or swords like all the other zealots in his time. Instead, he carried Truth, courage, compassion, raw supernatural power, and holy anger.

- He condemned religious systems.

In John 7, during the feast of Tabernacles, one of Israel's greatest annual events, Jesus stood up in the temple in Jerusalem and screamed out, "If anyone is thirsty, come to me and drink." (John 7:37) Can you picture what this looked like? Jesus stood up in the middle of Israel's "mega-church," while it was chock-full of "believers," and basically said, "I know you are unsatisfied with the religious system you're in. So come to me and I will give you what you've always been looking for. If you put your trust in me, I will cause rivers of living water to come out of you to quench your thirst in such a way that you will never thirst again." (John 7:37-38, paraphrase)

Then on one occasion, while some were giving Jesus a tour of the temple, the venerated center of religious activity and worship, he basically said, "It's all gonna come down." (Matthew 24:1-2; Mark 13:1-2; Luke 21:5-6) So, Jesus didn't care for the things that were honored by the pious people of his day. Instead, he knew that the death of its trappings would be its downfall.

Also, unlike many "Christians" today, Jesus didn't evangelize people to bring them to church, but to his Father and his friends and family who shared life with him. He wasn't about "the church" but about the kingdom of God lived in the earth, in word and deed, in every area of everyday life, through vulnerable, revolutionary relationships. And unlike so many "leaders" today, Jesus never gave a single thought to "church growth" or "membership" or "attendance." To him, it was never about "the numbers," as if his success was measured by such petty things.

He openly rebuked and embarrassed the "pastors," "reverends," and "men of God" to such a degree that they wanted to take him out by any means possible (Matthew 5:20; 12:9-14, 22-45; 15:1-14; 16:1-4; 19:2-9; 21:23-46; 22:15-23:39. Luke 12:1-12; 16:14-31; 20:1-47. Mark 7:6-16; 8:11-12; 10:2-9; 11:27-33; 12:35-40. John 8:14-30). He was a walking contradiction to everything the religious leaders lived for, and he never once complimented them – not once! Though the "church" looked "successful" on the surface, impressive for all to see, Jesus was still moved with pity when he saw things as they really were, when he saw the multitudes who were fainting and scattered like sheep without a shepherd (Matthew 9:35-38). The machinery of "churchianity" was impressive and magnificent, but not to Jesus. And a time even came when Jesus became so unmanageable that the Pharisees and Sadducees had to join forces to gang up on Jesus, which still didn't work (Matthew 22:34).

- He had what the "big-dogs" lacked and everyone knew it (Matthew 21:14-17; Mark 11:18). His life – everything he said and did – set him apart from the pretenders.

For example, have you ever considered how many times Jesus exorcised demons in "church"? (See Mark 1:21-28, 39; Luke 4:31-37; 13:10-17) And isn't it interesting that those demons possessed "church-goers," without fear in "the church," and without regard for the religious rulers? Obviously, those evil spirits didn't recognize their authority at all. And yet, when Jesus walked in, they trembled. Why? Because they feared him; they knew who he was while the clerics (who were themselves, possessed by religious spirits) remained clueless from day one.

Even the everyday person sensed something special about him that they had never noticed in their "pastors," "bishops," and super-duper, glow-in-the-dark "apostles." While the religious leaders cared more about sound doctrine, adherence to the law, reputation, political correctness, and well-formed sermons but lacked the authority to heal and deliver the hurting, Jesus loved so deeply that he had the power to get the job done every time. He didn't just talk the talk, he lived it and demonstrated the power of it, which set him apart from everyone else as one who had authority, whose words were "gracious...with power." (Luke 4:16-22, 31-44)

- He never once ranted about "going to church" or getting involved in "church" activities or routines. Why? Because he knew it wasn't necessary in the Kingdom. His own relationship with our Father wasn't dependent, in any way, on "church attendance," and when he did "go to church," he didn't do so to "get fed" or encouraged or to praise and worship in a collective body of believers or to become a better Christian. He simply lived out of his unbroken intimacy with his Father and his identity in him everywhere he went. And when it came to fellowship, he didn't "forsake the assembling" of himself together with "believers." (Hebrews 10:25, KJV) His relationship with "the people of God" was a part of His whole life. He walked arm-in-arm with his Father and everyone around him because, to him, they were all one family, 24/7. So, for someone to reprimand him for "not bein' in church" would have been pathetic, to say the least.

Needless to say, Jesus was not your average "church-going Christian." Most of the leaders labeled him a blasphemer (Matthew 26:57-66) while the crowds tried to make him king (John 6:15). And yet, it seems that no one really liked him – not really – because, in the end, Jesus was abandoned (John 10:24-39). After doing so many good things that even the world itself could not contain the books that could be written about them, Jesus was forsaken by all but a handful of people (Matthew 27:55-57; Mark 15:40-41; John 19:25-26; 21:25).

Of course, there were some religious "leaders" who believed in Jesus for a while, but they didn't go public because they didn't want to make any waves and certainly didn't want to be "kicked out" of the "church." Why? Because they loved the approval of men more than the approval of God (John 12:42-43). And then again, there were some "leaders" – very few in number – like Jairus, who knew Jesus had the goods and weren't too proud to ask him for help; they were too desperate for "more" of God to be concerned about anything other than their need of what he had (Mark 5:21-42; Luke 8:41-56).

The Nicolaitans

Jesus hated and spoke out against "the deeds of the Nicolaitans," the teachings, practices, and influence of those who "conquer" and "destroy" (nicos) "the people" (laity) (Revelation 2:6, 15-16). And what's sad is that these people, who thought they were "of God" and constantly declared their devotion to him, had no idea they were actually working against him. While Jesus came to bring freedom and restoration, these self-appointed clerics made themselves "lords over God's heritage" and bound them to religious rules and regulations. While Jesus came to serve and give his life, these wolves in sheep's clothing produced a subtle system of control and manipulation wherein they were fulfilled. While Jesus was busy about his Father's business, these "ministers" cared about building their "ministries," furthering their agenda, and inflating their wallets. While Jesus brought people into the liberty of love, grace, and truth, his opponents forced people into the darkness of fear, guilt, shame, and lies.

> Jesus saw the evil that was destroying the people he loved, and it was this love that motivated him to war against it so violently.

The Nicolaitans didn't really love people the way they should have, even though they thought they did. Though they may have thought they cared for God's children as good parents do, their actions spoke louder than their words. Deep inside, at the core of their hearts, they loved themselves and the bells and whistles that came with being the heads of a system that had nothing to do with God. And instead of spending themselves on broken humanity, they used and abused the masses to fund their plans, to erect bigger and better monuments, and to elevate themselves. The reason they hated Jesus was because he threatened everything they loved and worshipped. He saw the true intentions of their hearts, which even they could not see, and exposed them to the sunlight.

This is why Jesus didn't have one good thing to say about them and, in no uncertain terms, warned his disciples and everyone else against them (Matthew 16:6-12; 23:1-12; Luke 12:1-12; 22:24-28). He saw the evil that was destroying the people he loved, and it was this love that motivated him to war against it so violently (John 2:17; 8:12-59).

Final Thoughts

Today, most Christians measure their relationship to the Lord by the level of their relationship and commitment to a local church and by the type of church they attend; and this is how they judge others as well. But, if we measured Jesus by this same standard, he would fail our test.

But, I wonder, what would Jesus be like if he visited your church or the average church today? What would he do? Would your pastor like him and invite him to preach at his or her church?

Jesus' daily life with his friends and family has nothing to do with Christianity as it is known and practiced today; in fact, the gap between the two is enormous and compelling. And he certainly didn't intend for his life to spawn a religion that's based on building programs, denominationalism, hierarchal leadership models, non-profit organizations, church attendance, dogma, easy-believism, etc. Those who think otherwise would have to lift certain verses and passages out of the New Testament narrative, paste them together outside of their context, and add their spin in order to make their case.

Why does it matter so much to us where we meet, when we meet, and how we meet? Jesus didn't care a whit about church services and never said anything about how we ought to do church, and there is a very good reason for this: He wanted his friends to be free to focus on his ultimate purpose for them.

His way of doing everything was free and spontaneous because he knew that the wineskin, the structure and container of his life, had to be able to ebb and flow and flex with him and his assignment. Plus, his purpose took different forms and applications all the time, depending on where he was and who he was with. This is why he said, "Judge every tree by its fruit," not "Judge every tree by its bark" or "Judge every tree by its limb formation" or "Judge every tree by its width and height." To him, the end justified the means even when, to the natural mind, the means seemed counterproductive to the end. His life in his Father was never organized or restricted by man-made rules, rituals, and regulations. He simply lived holistically and organically out of the overflow of his relationship with his Father.

And it never mattered whether Jesus was in a house, temple or grain field, on a seashore, walkway or roadside. His Kingdom was relevant everywhere, everyday, with everyone. Indeed, there are many times in the Gospels where the authors never mention where Jesus was when he was teaching, healing, preaching, or whatever. Why? Because it simply did not matter.

Jesus loved people, valued personal relationships, and looked for every opportunity to fellowship with the broken, hungry, hurting, tormented, and rejected. This is why he spent so much time with people around the dinner table; he loved the atmosphere of transparency and vulnerability it produced, and it seemed to be one of the primary places where everyone could be themselves without fear. This life was his "church life."

What if Jesus became our pattern? Wouldn't our whole life become spiritually sacred and alive through and through? What if we lived like the Church of Jesus Christ that we are, instead of merely going to church? Would our 9 to 5 jobs not become more meaningful? Would our homes not become more heavenly? What if we all became personally responsible for our own spiritual lives and depended more on the Lord to be our shepherd, rather than a mere human being?

Recent statistics from *The Barna Group* and *Pew Research* show that most churched Christians are immature and fruitless when compared to those who do not go to church but have a personal relationship with Jesus and his people and maintain a healthy, disciplined, balanced diet in the Word of God and prayer. Of course, Jesus' disciples had their own relationship with the Lord and each other and kept themselves "spiritually" fit by spending time with him and studying the Scriptures and look how mature they were, compared to their religious counterparts. They lived as a community of faith and love out of the overflow of their individual love-affairs with the Lord and it spread into every area of life until the whole world was turned upside down.

> Most churched Christians are immature and fruitless when compared to those who do not go to church but have a personal relationship with Jesus and his people and maintain a healthy, disciplined, balanced diet in the Word of God and prayer.

Wherever two or more are gathered together, in his name, he is there with them. This was and still is Jesus' definition of "church" and does not need to be improved upon. As for whether or not you should go to church or not is between you and him – no one can tell you that. The venue does not matter and never has. What matters is that we each have our own relationship with him and that we have deep, meaningful fellowship with one another as he brings us together in his life, by his spirit.

Recommended Reading:

- *So You Don't Want To Go To Church Anymore* by Wayne Jacobsen
- *Pagan Christianity* by Frank Viola & George Barna

- 6 -

The Riddler

A s I think about the church today, it seems the preaching of
sermons is a centerpiece to the faith (Ironically, this has also
been true throughout church history). Pulpit-based ministers are
constantly graded by how graceful, logical, and clear they are, as
well as by the stories they tell to further illustrate their
monologues. But after studying homiletics (the art of preaching)
and various public speaking resources and comparing them to
Jesus' life, I cannot help but notice some major distinctions.

Let me explain...

After thousands of years of living under the darkness and pain of
The Fall, Jesus came on the scene with the greatest message of all
time: "the Kingdom of God is here. Repent and believe." This
was the Gospel of the Kingdom. This was his message, his
purpose, his calling: to preach this Good News to the poor, to
seek and save those who are lost (Mark 1:38; Luke 4:43; 7:22;
19:10).

But there was a problem...

He communicated with allegories and dark speech (Psalm 78:2;
Matthew 13:34-35; Mark 4:33-34). I like what Aiden W. Tozer
once said, "Preachers' illustrations were given to throw light and
illustrate, where many of the parables of Jesus were given for the
purpose of obscuring truth." In other words, Jesus' riddled words
veiled Truth from the merely curious and stimulated the inquiry
of the really concerned, confusing most (if not all) of his hearers,
leaving them with more questions than answers. Then, when he

was asked to explain his allegories, he sometimes would, but it rarely helped.

And if that wasn't enough...

1) He frequently addressed multiple topics in one long-winded message, thousands of years before the invention of the 4 hour chair.
2) He often devastated his audiences by saying things no one else would ever say that were hard if not impossible to accept, leaving the people offended (Matthew 8:18-22; Luke 11:29-32; 14:25-35).
3) He would answer questions with questions (Or, better yet, he would answer them with more symbolic stories or anecdotes).
4) He would repeat himself, using a different parable when his audience didn't understand what he was trying to say with his first, second or third parables.

Today leaders do all they can to improve the appeal, clarity, and entertainment value of their messages, but Jesus was a different kind of communicator. If he knew anything about the art of preaching or public speaking, he certainly didn't show it.

But why did Jesus talk like this? Was he simply trying to be different, or was he just trying to be difficult? Did he like being misunderstood? Did he not care about improving his chances of success or broadening his circle of influence? What about the popular majority? Didn't Jesus have a board of directors or "headquarters" to keep him on track? Whatever happened to meeting your listeners where they are, on their level? If Jesus was a man of God, would he not have been more sympathetic and loving in

> Did Jesus not read Daius Carnegus' book, "How to Win Jews and Influence Greeks"?

his delivery? Did he not read Daius Carnegus' book, "How to Win Jews and Influence Greeks"?

Who would have thought that God would come in the flesh in an effort to restore all things but would do it all wrong, so contrary to conventional wisdom? And yet there was something alive in his words that touched people deep inside where no one had ever touched them before. Every word carried grace and truth inside it, astonishing some and terrifying others, stirring the desperate, freeing the bound, and healing the broken.

Many wondered, "How is it that this man has learning...when he has never studied?" (John 7:15, Amp; see also Matthew 13:54; Mark 1:22). Where did his boldness, authority, knowledge and wisdom come from? He had no degrees or credentials from any school or university and he wasn't ordained by any religious organizations. He didn't present theories or philosophies with "excellence of speech" but spoke the wisdom of God in a mystery. His preaching and teaching was not presented with persuasive words of human wisdom but in demonstration of the Spirit and power, so people's faith would not rest on human ability but in the power of God. He only spoke what he heard his Father say, as he heard his Father speak (Matthew 10:27 and John 5:19, 30; 8:25-29, 38; 12:49-50; 14:10, 24, 31). This is why those who were naturally-minded rejected his teachings. His words were non-sense to them (1 Corinthians 2, Amp).

He was like an alien in this world who spoke every language but those of the people around him. He didn't think or communicate like everyone else because his mind and heart were constantly preoccupied with Kingdom matters, influencing his interactions with everyone and everything, everyday. As C. S. Lewis once said, "A man who was merely a man and said the sort of things Jesus said would not be a great moral teacher. He would either be a lunatic - on a level with the man who says he is a poached egg - or else he would be the Devil of hell. You must make your choice. Either this man was and is the Son of God, or else a madman or something worse."

To an oppressed people yearning for freedom from Roman rule, he gave startling advice, such as, "If an enemy soldier orders you to walk a mile with him, walk two, and if he slaps you on one cheek, offer the other." He would also tell them things like, "Rejoice in persecution" and "Be grateful for your poverty." His unbending principles and absolutist qualities left everyone gasping for air, confused and perhaps outraged - not comforted.

It's easy to criticize someone for being contrary to the way we think things should be done, but how do we know our way is best? Jesus could have met people where they were but how would that have helped? There is more knowledge in the earth today than has ever been, and there are more ways to communicate truth than have ever existed, but are we better for it? In the end, it all comes down to having a deep and personal love for Truth, and only those who love Truth will seek it, even to their own hurt. Jesus baited everyone with veiled, offensive Truth, and said, "Blessed...is he who takes no offense at me and finds no cause for stumbling in or through me and is not hindered from seeing the Truth." (Matthew 11:6, Amp) The internal struggle that takes place deep within our hearts and minds when we are confronted with Truth must be embraced, not shunned, and we are the only ones who are responsible for casting the deciding vote in favor of Truth. Of course, this can be a very hard process, but when we want the freedom and liberty that comes from his reality more than the false comfort of what we've always felt and believed, we will run to him, away from everything that's not him.

A Holocaustic Homily

As I've spent the last couple of years dissecting the four Gospels, I've been intrigued, for one thing, by Jesus' "sermons," all of which would have a dramatic, negative effect on the average person today. One message that rocked me in more ways than one is in John 6. As you will see, Jesus had an agenda to fulfill, even if it meant losing popularity.

According to this chapter, on one particular day a huge crowd (larger than 5000 people) was following Jesus, drawn to him by the miracles, signs and wonders he had performed. Knowing the people were physically hungry after following him for quite some time, he multiplied five loaves of bread and two fishes and fed them until they were full. Of course, this so impressed the people that they tracked him down a little later, hoping he would repeat the miracle and feed them a second time.

However, Jesus didn't give them what they wanted. His reason for multiplying the food the first time was to keep the crowd from starving, but this time he had something much better in mind.

So, in response to their request, he said, "Stop toiling and doing and producing for the food that perishes and decomposes...but strive and work and produce rather for the [lasting] food which endures [continually] unto life eternal; the Son of Man will give (furnish) you that, for God the father has authorized and certified him and put his seal of endorsement upon him." (John 6:27, Amp)

What was Jesus talking about? Didn't he understand what these people wanted? Didn't he understand that you have to please people to keep them around? Evidently, he wasn't too sensitive to their needs, and he certainly didn't know how to talk to them because what he said went right over their heads. We know this because they then asked a question that had nothing to do with what he was talking about (John 6:28). Then, after answering their question, which again didn't meet their satisfaction, they asked him, "What sign...will you perform then, so that we may see it and believe and rely on and adhere to you? What [supernatural] work have you [to show what you can do]?" (John 6:30, Amp) These people were incorrigible and were so desperate for food and a "show" that they asked him to rain manna out of heaven like Moses did for the children of Israel in the desert.

But Jesus replied, "Moses did not give you the bread from heaven...but it is my father who gives you the true heavenly bread." (John 6:32, Amp)

This confused the people even more because they still thought he was talking about literal bread (John 6:34). They were physically hungry and Jesus was talking about heavenly food and he wasn't even hinting at feeding them after "church." Instead, he proceeded to talk about this strange, mysterious bread and would intersperse even stranger statements about himself such as when he identified himself as "the bread of life" and told them, "If anyone eats of this bread, he will live forever." (John 6:51, Amp)

Of course, this upset the Jews who thought he was talking about cannibalism; they even started fighting among themselves. It would've been nice if Jesus had merely explained himself, but he didn't. He just kept preaching and then, to make matters worse, he made a statement that was even more unsettling:

"...You cannot have any life in you unless you eat the flesh of the Son of Man and drink his blood...He who feeds on my flesh and drinks my blood has...eternal life, and I will raise him up...on the last day. For my flesh is true and genuine food, and my blood is true and genuine drink. He who feeds on my flesh and drinks my blood dwells continually in me, and I...in him. Just as the living father sent me and I live by (through, because of) the father, even so whoever continues to feed on me [whoever takes me for his food and is nourished by me] shall [in his turn] live through and because of me. This is the bread that came down from heaven...he who takes this bread for his food shall live forever." (John 6:53-58, Amp)

108

Now, how many of us, if we had been there, hearing this message, would have given Jesus a piece of our mind? Can you imagine your reaction? How would you respond? This was definitely the kind of message that begged clarification but was "lost in translation."

> If Jesus really loved those people, he would have spoken to them on their level, right?

Think about it - if Jesus really loved those people, he would have spoken to them on their level, right? He would have been more "seeker sensitive," more compassionate, more considerate; he would have read his audience and met them where they were, on their level. Am I wrong?

How many of us would have said something like...

"Jesus, we know you're the Son of God, and we don't want to presume to tell you what to do, but can you be more practical? We have no idea what you're talking about. Keep it simple. Don't be so super-spiritual, so mysterious. We're 'average' folks you know. Don't you think it would help if you spoke more plainly? Just say what you mean. If we can't understand what you're saying, what good is it?"

I can even hear some religious leaders saying...

"Jesus, I've been in ministry a long time. Let me give you some advice. When you're in Rome, be as the Romans. Speak to them on their level. Don't talk over their heads. If you keep this up the crowds won't come back to your meetings. Your reputation will plummet and attendance will drop, and you know what that means: no more tithes and offerings. Is that really what you want? Oh, and by the way, your message was very arrogant. Who do you think you are? You need some humility. Let me pray for you."

If Jesus were alive today, as he was in John 6, how would we perceive him? Would we praise his "ministry" as being "fruitful" and "effective"? Would we see him the way heaven does or would we only see him through our own eyes?

Jesus was gentle and humble in heart but not like we think. We think confusion only comes from satan which is why we blame the enemy every time "confusion" shows up. We think that being offensive is unkind and unloving, but Jesus served as he was directed by our Father. This is why we must learn to know and judge after the Spirit (the heart) and not the flesh (2 Corinthians 5:16). We must see the heart of every person and every matter with the eyes of our hearts.

Jesus was offering the multitudes the greatest gift he could ever give: himself, his flesh and blood, his very Life! And yet Jesus wrapped his gift in ambiguous, cannibalistic, pagan language (e.g. "Eat my flesh" and "Drink my blood"), and no one liked it. And as a result, he didn't just rock the boat - he sunk it! He offered them another level of communion (relationship) with himself with strong and offensive words that brought everyone up short. Even many of his own disciples were upset. They said, "This is a hard and difficult and strange saying (an offensive and unbearable message). Who can stand to hear it? [Who can be expected to listen to such teaching?]." (John 6:60, Amp)

But Jesus wasn't their kind of Messiah. He didn't meet their needs and provide circuses on demand. So the large and restless crowd filed away. The feeding of the multitudes attracted thousands, which is a "good thing" to those who crave success, but when he opened his "unsanctified" mouth, they split. Why? Because they followed him for his works, not his words; they wanted what he had, not who he was.

Jesus' sermon was like a T-bone steak to a new-born baby, like trying to fit a square peg through a round hole; it was too hard to swallow. And he knew it, which is why he asked his disciples, "Is this a stumbling block and an offense to you? [Does this upset and displease and shock and scandalize you?]." (John 6:61, Amp)

His words were Spirit and Life and could not be understood apart from his Spirit and faith in him (John 6:63-64). But Jesus wasn't surprised or discouraged when most of his followers deserted him and went back to their old lives and associations (John 6:66). He knew no one could follow him on their own unless they were enabled by our Father. This is why he didn't beat himself up for preaching the way he did. He simply delivered the message he was given by our Father and trusted him to do the rest. He knew he was only the vessel, not the source.

> Jesus' disciples didn't react out of pain when he shined light on their darkness or raised the standard on their lives. They abandoned their need for self-preservation enough to keep a tight hold on him when everyone else was running away.

Jesus' message turned up the heat and drove everyone away except his original disciples. Why? They could have easily followed everyone else, but they didn't. When Jesus asked them if they too would leave him, Peter answered, "Lord, to whom shall we go? You have the words...of eternal life." (John 6:68, Amp) In other words, they discerned that Jesus was the only one whose words made them come alive; they no longer had any confidence in the religious system of their day. When Jesus spoke, their hearts burned within them. He had something they wanted, and they were too desperate to be critical, easily offended, or scared away by what they didn't understand.

The Inner Circle

Despite popular opinion, Jesus didn't treat everyone the same. Within the ranks of the multitudes who "followed" him, he had an inner circle – his disciples – with whom he shared more revelation (Mark 4:10-12, 34). He spoke in code to the crowds but gave his disciples a little more light than the rest. I say "a little more light" because even being on the inside track, they were still often confused and distressed by most of what he said (Matthew 19:25; Luke 18:31-34; John 4:31-38; 11:8-10). And sometimes they were too afraid to ask him what he was talking about. Why? Because he would often rebuke them for their dullness and lack of faith (Matthew 15:17; 16:5-12; Mark 4:13; 7:18; 8:14-21; 9:30-32; Luke 9:43-45).

Jesus did not make it easy or comfortable for his disciples to follow him and yet they stayed with him because they knew he had more, and was more, than anyone they knew. They didn't react out of pain when Jesus shined light on their darkness or raised the standard on their lives. They abandoned their need for self-preservation enough to keep a tight hold on him when everyone else was running away.

Go Get It!

Jesus preached, taught, and conversed as he was directed by our Father, and no one understood him except those who had ears to hear, eyes to see, and hearts to understand (Matthew 11:15; 13:9, 13-16, 43; Mark 4:9-11; 6:52; 7:16). His words were veiled to those who did not believe, whose minds were blinded by the god of this age (2 Corinthians 4:3-4). He spoke mysteries in mysterious ways to a spiritually deaf and dull generation. Many hung on his every word while others, especially the religious leaders and crowds, were enraged to the point of plotting his death. Yet, he wasn't moved.

On one particular occasion, when Jesus was speaking to a crowd of people who did not understand his words, he explained why they were so dull:

"I tell the things which I have seen and learned at my father's side, and your actions also reflect what you have heard and learned from your father...If God were your father, you would love me and respect me and welcome me gladly, for I proceeded (came forth) from God [out of his very presence]. I did not even come on my own authority or of my own accord (as self-appointed); but he sent me. Why do you misunderstand what I say? It is because you are unable to hear what I am saying. [You cannot bear to listen to my message; your ears are shut to my teaching.] You are of your father, the devil, and it is your will to practice the lusts and gratify the desires [which are characteristic] of your father. He was a murderer from the beginning and does not stand in the truth, because there is no truth in him. When he speaks a falsehood, he speaks what is natural to him, for he is a liar [himself] and the father of lies and of all that is false. But because I speak the truth, you do not believe me [do not trust me, do not rely on me, or adhere to me]. Who of you convicts me of wrongdoing or finds me guilty of sin? Then if I speak truth, why do you not believe me [trust me, rely on, and adhere to me]? Whoever is of God listens to God. [Those who belong to God hear the words of God.] This is the reason that you do not listen [to those words, to me]: because you do not belong to God and are not of God or in harmony with him." (John 8:38, 42-47, Amp)

Then, in John 10:26-27, he told another group, "...You do not believe and trust and rely on me because you do not belong to my fold [you are no sheep of mine]. The sheep that are my own hear and are listening to my voice; and I know them, and they follow me." (Amp)

Everything Jesus said was Spirit and Life, hidden from the wise and learned and revealed only to the childlike: those who were trusting, lowly, loving, and forgiving (Matthew 11:25-27; John 6:63; Proverbs 1:23; 1 Corinthians 2:9-16). Therefore, Jesus placed the responsibility for understanding his words upon his hearers (Matthew 19:11-12; Luke 8:18). He never cast his pearls to pigs and never gave holy things to dogs (Matthew 7:6). Rather, he sowed his seed on the ground of humanity, expecting a harvest from those whose hearts were as the richest soil, hungry and desperate for him.

> Jesus used parables…rather than easy answers and obvious explanations, to entice his hearers into a deeper, more inter-active relationship with him and his world.

He shrouded his Truths in smoke and mirrors because "it is the glory of God to conceal a thing: but the honor of kings is to search out a matter." (Proverbs 25:2. See also Revelation 1:6) Jesus used parables to conceal truth for those who were spiritually hungry enough to invest themselves in an imaginative pursuit for meaning. He used this method, rather than easy answers and obvious explanations, to entice his hearers into a deeper, more inter-active relationship with him and his world.

As Bill Johnson says, "God doesn't hide things from you, he hides things for you." The mysteries of the Kingdom have been wrapped in layers, like an onion, waiting for those who have the essential passion and guts to start peeling, as long as it takes, to get to the heart of the "matter." He has placed gold, silver and precious gems in rocks and caves and said, "If you want it, go get it!" He wants us to discover his treasures, but he isn't going to make it easy for us. Why? Because we will not value what we do not pay for. Also, we cannot be trusted with his resources until we have developed the needed character within us to responsibly steward what we find. This is why, from heaven's viewpoint, the journey is as important as the destination; the process of exploration is as significant as the discovery itself.

Talk Like God

What if we followed Jesus' example? What if we only spoke what we heard our Father say? Would we talk more or less? Would our words not be more profound, more edifying, more eternal?

Am I encouraging parabolic preaching over clear-cut, three-point sermons? Do I think we should talk in code all the time, using riddles, telling stories and answering questions with questions? Am I discouraging socially relevant oratory methods and styles? Absolutely not! Christianity isn't about mimicking what Jesus said in the Gospels, verbatim. We're not parrots or robots! Our Father doesn't want us to be like Jesus in every single way, just like no loving parent wants their younger children to be just like their oldest sibling. We are all unique and every situation we face is different.

The core principle of Jesus' life is very simple: In every situation, at every fork in the road, he sought our Father's heart and only spoke what he heard our Father say (John 7:16; 8:26, 28, 38; 12:49-50; 14:10). He never left room for anything but his Father's influence. He never went to school to learn public speaking or the art of preaching. Of course, this isn't to say that formal oratory training isn't beneficial; there are times when we may be lead by our Father to educate ourselves in this way. But when our focus is more on connecting with people, with our audiences or congregations, than it is on hearing and obeying our Father, we have strayed from the simplicity of devotion to Christ. "Seeker sensitivity" should never become more important than being sensitive to our Father's heart. Jesus lived to show us how to live, like a little child, dependent on our Daddy for his wisdom for each and every situation. As a result, he lived out of the wisdom and strength of God, putting the wisdom and strength of man to shame.

What if we flushed out every thought or concern in our heads that allows peer pressure to have any say in what we say and how we say it? What if we simply stopped caring about pleasing ourselves and everyone else? What if we spoke as if only one Person was listening? Would we not speak Life? Why do we fret about what things may sound like to so-n-so? How can we ever live the true Christian life when we still care so much about being liked by mere men?

Those who have set their hearts on following Jesus, as he followed our dear Father, will see his fruit in their lives. Like Jesus, their words will be powerful and profound, offending the religious, restoring the broken, freeing the bound, feeding the hungry, and shaking the nations as they hear and speak the words of God from his lips.

"*People talk about imitating Christ, and imitate Him in the little trifling formal things, such as washing the feet, saying His prayer, and so on; but if anyone attempts the real imitation of Him, there are no bounds to the outcry with which the presumption of that person is condemned.*"
Florence Nightingale

For more resources from *Inner Life Media*
visit *InnerLifeMinistries.com*

www.ingramcontent.com/pod-product-compliance
Lightning Source LLC
Chambersburg PA
CBHW030047100426
42734CB00036B/425